**The Adventurous Montrealer's
Food Guide**

*To as great a degree as sexuality,
food is inseparable from the imagination.*

Jean-François Revel

JoAnn Issenman

The Adventurous Montrealer's Food Guide

© 1988, Tundra Books Inc.

Published in Canada by Tundra Books, Montreal,
Quebec H3G 1R4

Published in the United States by Tundra Books of
Northern New York, Plattsburgh, NY 12901

Canadian Cataloguing in Publication Data

Issenman, JoAnn Masson, 1945-
The adventurous Montrealer's food guide

Includes index.

ISBN 0-88776-229-8

1. Grocery trade—Quebec (Province)—Montreal—
Directories. 2. Ethnic food industry—Quebec (Province)—
Montreal—Directories. I. Title.

HD9325.C33M6 1988 381'.456413'0025714281
C-88-090305-8

Frontispiece: *New owner John Porter takes over
The Cheese Shoppe — one of Canada's first and
longest lasting.*

Cover and interior photos: Laureen Sweeney, Montreal
Design: Rolf Harder & Associates Inc., Montreal

Printed in Canada

To my mother whose enthusiasm
for food and the markets of New York
inspired this adventure

Contents

Preface

This book is a celebration of the people who make sausages, bake bread, hand dip chocolate, roast coffee and put food on our table. Some came from distant places, some were born in Canada. This book is an invitation to patronize these Montreal shopkeepers and to appreciate their art, their cuisine and, often, their culture.

It was not my intention to discover the best of this or that; although some discoveries are the "best," others are the "only." Some shops are elegant and others a bit shabby. Some of the shops have memorable products, others do not; but each provoked my interest in some way. Perhaps it was the fact that an artisan sausage-maker still used the machinery, methods and

recipes brought from the old country. Or perhaps it was a pastry-maker committed to excellence in ingredients, freshness and presentation. Or a friendly shopkeeper with an exotic product from a distant or disappearing world. I set about to meet people who preserve a culture, a food tradition, and who add to our city's culinary heritage.

While writing this book, I often felt that I was in a race against time. Could I write the book faster than Harvey's, McDonald's or Provi-Soir would replace a newly discovered Portuguese barbecue or a Chilean immigrant's infant restaurant? Would I beat the creeping gentrification in inner-city neighborhoods to record the history of a beloved Polish bakery? Would the yuppies march up from St. Denis Street and swallow La Binerie Mont Royal after fifty years? Will our children experience the taste of fresh fish or only a "nugget" extruded from a machine?

This is a resource book for people who like food and enjoy the hunt. It's a book to help you discover Montreal. Above all, it's a book about people.

A Note:

If you plan to make a special trip to any one of these stores, do phone ahead. I haven't included store hours or days as they seem to change so often. Some places are closed on Sundays, others on Mondays. Check.

Opposite: Service with a smile at Phoenicia Adonis

Bakeries

Montreal has the most extraordinary range of bakeries and pastry shops of any city in North America, in part a reflection of our ethnic mosaic and in part due to the seriousness with which we take our bread and cake. French bread aficionados claim that the best baguettes in North America — the ones that remain truest to the Parisian taste — can be found in Montreal. Whether that be true or not, it is possible to find everything from good, chewy Armenian bread to Chilean *colisa* to smoky, whole-wheat Greek breads.

We are blessed with a few true artisans of cake and pastry — people with magic hands who create éclairs, kugelhupfs, and moon cakes out of butter, flour, cream and eggs. People who satisfy our sinful cravings for sweets and send us away with divine white boxes tied with pastel ribbons and stiff white bags with promising butter stains.

The savoury and the sweet at Franni's

Canadian

Franni Pâtisseries-Cafés
5528 Monkland Avenue
N.D.G. H4A 1C7
486-2033

Franni Sheper is the Cheesecake Queen of Montreal. She's earned her title cracking 20,000 dozen eggs and beating sixteen tons of cream cheese a year. A lady who loves her work . . . an ebullient ambassador of cheesecake. And what cheesecake it is — always lush, always seductive, always subtly flavored — Baileys Irish Cream, Gianduja, Nocciola and just plain.

And the cakes. The Tweed chocolate cake, served with a velvet chocolate sauce . . . the Madonna chocolate cake, made with egg whites and no flour . . . the chocolate mousse cake. Chocolate fantasies — made with deep, dark Callebaut chocolate shipped from Belgium.

There are Linzertortes — a basketweave of pastry carefully laid over bright red raspberry jam. The amazing Apple Nut Crisp Torte which seems to defy the law of gravity as it builds to a mound of carefully arranged apple slices — and always served with thick whipped cream. From an old family recipe, pecan buns are the stickiest, most pecan-y in the world.

Jorge Koc, known as "Koqui," is the chef at Franni's. He's responsible for the savory items — a good vegetable lasagna, a high custardy quiche, homey, robust soups.

Franni is a lady who loves her work — she understands baking intuitively. Her husband and partner, Wally, says she has a natural feel for creating cakes and rarely needs two tries to achieve perfection. If perfection can be measured by long lines at the takeout counter, perfection has been achieved.

Kilo
5206 St. Laurent Boulevard
Montreal H2T 1X1
277-5039

While your dieting friends are visiting Multigrains Bakery, sneak across the street to Kilo. Steal away with a piece or two of blueberry torte, oozing plump fresh berries. A mountainous apple torte cannot be ignored. The pies are particularly well constructed — artfully crimped and arranged. Cheesecakes come in cappuccino, pineapple, chocolate — a multitude of mortal sins — all dense, lush and irresistible. Try the Italian gelati — smooth, fruity and not overly sweet. Penny candy is sold by the kilo and devotees are not just kids. Whole cakes and pies should be ordered in advance.

Logan's Bakery
1024 Jean Talon West
Montreal H3N 1T1
272-9517

Logan's at the age of one hundred qualifies as a Montreal institution. Generations of children have savored the jam and date turnovers, Logan's special jelly rolls and their tiny mincemeat tarts. Where else in Montreal can you get Eccles, those particularly British puff pastry confections filled with currants and raspberry jam; where else, a steady supply of hot cross buns, cheese bread, oatmeal bread, graham-flour scones? Dainty, perfect fist-sized tourtières. Hovis bread made with wheat germ and bran . . . the same recipe for one hundred years.

Mr. and Mrs. James Wood took over from Mr. Wood's uncle in 1945. They deserve their Sundays off. (A smaller selection of Logan's baked goods is available in Ogilvy's basement, 1307 St. Catherine Street West, H3G 1P7.)

Multigrains
5235 St. Laurent Boulevard
Montreal H2T 1S4
279-1102

This friendly bakery is the offspring of a marriage between a Jamaican and a French-Canadian. That explains the two teenage cousins, one black and one white, who man the weekend ovens. The visitor is invited to choose steaming hot loaves, just tapped out of their molds.

The Dyke family uses no preservatives or sugar in preparing their range of natural breads. Apple juice and molasses are used as sweeteners. Those on sugar-free or gluten-free diets can indulge in Multigrain cakes, muffins and specialties like "hardo" bread, a heavy white loaf favored in the Caribbean. Farm-fresh eggs are available here. The weekday baker prepares a healthy vegetarian pizza to go. Don't overlook the whole-wheat hamburger rolls.

Nothing Fancy
5962 Monkland Avenue
N.D.G. H4A 1G9
482-7936

"Nothing fancy" is a Maritime expression that translates into "simple but good." Karon Anne Meikle of Parkdale, P.E.I., started baking at the age of six. She uses recipes left to her by her grandmother — recipes that, by the way, have no measurements. Islanders are paranoid about recording their recipes because of the intense competition at the annual baking fairs. Karon says that she does "head baking." And she isn't making too many mistakes. She says, "I do whatever you would do at home — home baking." Well, not my home.

Fragrant, whole-wheat cinnamon-raisin bread, currant-studded scones,

"Home baking" with Karon Anne at Nothing Fancy

"grandma's cookies," chocolate cheesecake muffins, Nanaimo bars stuffed with cream, maple muffins. Customers often bring their own baking pans to fill so they can "kinda lie." This down-home shop looks like a friendly Maritime kitchen. And Karon knows all the good P.E.I. gossip, too.

Pâtisserie St. Marc
2536 Beaubien Street East
Montreal H1Y 1G2
727-1313

With four generations of Cornelliers still baking here, Pâtisserie St. Marc is certainly an authentic family bakery and a Rosemount institution. It's not elegant, but it's comfortable and friendly. Nothing is particularly remarkable but everything is, rather, well-made in a homey sort of way. Good robust soups to go . . . pâté chinois, chicken and meat pies.

One of the few places in Montreal that make a decent sugar pie and a good-looking pecan pie. If you drop in here at holiday time – Easter, St. Valentine's Day, Mother's Day or Christmas – that's when the Cornellier family shines, producing a profusion of chocolate shapes, a fantasy of truffles, bunnies, hearts and Santas . . . a blizzard of chocolate.

Chinese

Pâtisserie Luong Huu
84 de La Gauchetière Street West
Montreal H2Z 1C1
397-9410

Pâtisserie Mei Heung
90 de La Gauchetière Street West
Montreal H2Z 1C1
875-6395

Far Eastern pastry is relatively unknown to Montrealers, but that should not last long. Two Oriental pastry shops have opened side by side on de La Gauchetière, both offering essentially the same repertoire. The Chinese do not end their meals with dessert.

Sweets and pastries are taken at various times during the day. Both shops have tables where one can relax with a cup of tea and sample the pastries. Chinese pastries are denser and eggier than Western pastries, often cloyingly sweet, but always marvelously subtle in their flavoring.

Try a sweet winter melon bun with sesame seed topping or a more familiar lemon tart. There are savory cakes which are used for the dim sum lunch — barbecued pork bun, curried beef bun, black bean bun. There are sweeter coconut and egg buns and black bean moon cakes. A light and fluffy egg and milk cream-cake, a Chinese éclair, is not to be missed.

French, traditional

La Boutique du Pâtissier
1075 Laurier Avenue West
Outremont H2V 2L2
279-5274

A large and gleaming pastry shop with a restaurant in the back. Good quality pastries, salads and breads. Exquisite fruit tarts. Hearty French breads dusted with flour. Classic French charcuterie salads and aspics.

Pâtisserie Belge
3485 Park Avenue
Montreal H2X 2H6
845-1245

A chic pastry-charcuterie in La Cité area. Partner in calories to Restaurant Chez Gautier which adjoins the shop. Well-made, fancy French cakes with glossy, glazed surfaces. Golden danoises for coffee — exquisite, carefully coiffed fruit tarts. Hearty French breads, in particular, a good whole-wheat loaf. Imported bulk Belgian chocolates. Dainty pâtes de fruits, gummy, sugary fruit-flavored candies. Pastel-colored sugared almonds for christenings. A selection of cheese and charcuterie that would make a Parisian nostalgic.

Pâtisserie de Gascogne
6095 Gouin Boulevard West
Cartierville H4J 1E7
331-0550

The true Montreal successor to the elegant, classic bejeweled Parisian pastry shop. No one who makes the voyage to Gouin Boulevard, hard by Belmont Park, comes away disappointed. The chic, the hard to please, the gourmands and gourmets of this city know Pâtisserie de Gascogne. Gascogne sets the standard that other shops must meet.

The stylish shop is temptation itself. Counters of homemade chocolate dotted with rows of foil-wrapped treasures. Pristine, orderly queues of marzipan "fruits." Racks of warm baguettes and crisp, buttery croissants. Counters brilliant with glazed and fruit-topped tarts.

The *bombes glacées* and the *entremets glacés* are among the wonders of Gascogne. The golden

brown Poire Williams — pear and raspberry sorbet shaped to resemble an Anjou pear. Or the Val d'Or — a confection of apricot and blueberry sorbet, studded with candied apricots and macaroons and perfumed with apricot brandy. Gascogne does memorable wedding cakes.

Prepared foods are frozen or ready to eat . . . chicken *basquaise* . . . *coq au vin*. Notable quiche . . . high, fluffy, custardy. "Vaut le voyage," as they would say in the Michelin Guide.

Pâtisserie Lenôtre Paris
1050 Laurier Avenue West
Outremont H2V 2K8
270-2702

One of Gaston Lenôtre's first outposts in the new world. The Paris-based pâtissier extraordinaire keeps a careful watch over his far-flung empire, checking that the puff pastry is perfectly puffed and the croissants are golden and buttery. The Groc family are the Montreal guardians of the famous name. Their army of pastry chefs turns out exquisite cakes, pastries, breads and sorbets.

Chocolates are flown in from Paris. Buy a small ballotin filled with assorted chocolates or an elaborate brocade-covered box of truffles.

Sweet seduction at Pâtisserie Lenôtre Paris

The pastries range from tiny, bejeweled petits fours to prim *religieuses* with nun-like shapes, filled with chocolate or coffee creams. A rainbow of sorbet-filled cups lines the counters. Bright lemon and orange halves filled with sorbet . . . cakes that are a glory to France. The chocolate-filled *Concorde* is topped with curls of chocolate dusted with sugar. The *feuille d'automne* is a chocolate génoise endowed with a superstructure of chocolate swirls.

A gourmet takeout changes daily — one day delicate quails with raisins; the next, rabbit in mustard sauce. Porcelain plates from Paris line the shelves along with treasures like *oranges confites au vodka*. A bit of the 16th Arrondissement come to Montreal.

Pâtisserie Mercier
200 Jarry Street East
Montreal H2P 1T5
387-1741

This busy corner of Jarry and St. Denis is home to an award-winning pastry shop. Michel Forget was winner of an award from the Confédération Nationale de la Pâtisserie-Confiserie-Glacerie of France. A very pretty shop that would look right at home in some well-bred Paris neighborhood. There are some good-looking pastries and homemade chocolates. To note: an almond "tulipe" cup filled with whipped cream and fruits.

Cooling racks of zytni, razowy, pleciona

Pâtisserie de Nancy
5655 Monkland Avenue
N.D.G. H4A 2Y6
482-3030

An elegant wood, tile and stone shop that would look at home in Nancy, in the Alsace region of France. Pâtisserie de Nancy does fruit tarts beautifully — ruby red strawberries under a shiny glaze or a mixed fruit tart with a bright kiwi border. Holiday time brings out armies of homemade chocolate bunnies, fish and Santas. The freezer holds difficult-to-make puff pastry for home bakers who want to save a step. Excellent bread. Try the *miche* — a good round, crusty loaf.

Le Relais de Sologne
2122 Drummond Street
Montreal H3G 1W9
843-6136

The Sologne, in the heart of France, was home to the brother and sister team of Chantal and Marc Leblanc. Their charming little step-down restaurant, in the shadow of the Ritz, is named for their home country. The Leblancs and their chef, Gérard Pinaud of Toulon, preside over a dozen pink-clothed tables. Marc bakes the bread and pastries, Gérard handles the savories and Chantal is the charming hostess.

Two refrigerated counters are artfully arranged with colorful pastries, homemade chocolates and light takeout meals. Try the quiche to take out . . . also a *manchon*, or "little muff," filled with ham and cheese. *Osso buco* or *blanquette de veau* can be warmed at home. The kitchen will prepare hors d'oeuvres and hot dishes for parties.

The signature of Le Relais is truly their distinctive pastries — most of which are covered in almond paste, highly decorated — small and delicious works of art. For a special present — a small "pot" of chocolate, filled with truffles.

Greek

Boulangerie Jimmy
4812 St. Urbain Street
Montreal H2T 2W2
270-2073

This 22-year-old neighborhood bakery is the secret weapon, literally behind, the Greek restaurants of Park Avenue. Try the round, crusty whole-wheat bread that the Symposium buys from Jimmy's. Jimmy Dimitri can be seen making the Greek pastries at the back of the store. Two of particular note — *bougaza*, a custard-filled crepe, and *galaktobouriko*, a golden semolina custard cake surrounded by flaky phyllo pastry. Take home a few thick slices of sesame bar for your lunch bag.

Boulangerie et Pâtisserie Samos
4379 St. Laurent Boulevard
Montreal H2W 1Z8
845-8033

Uptown ladies on their way to Waldman's have long known the secrets of Samos Greek bakery. Look for a window display jammed with festive blue and pink meringues and armies of Black Forest cakes. If there's a line-up, join it. Pick up a few crusty, fat rolls attached like a chain, or flat, round whole-wheat bread with a thick crust dusted with flour, which some claim is better than you can find in Greece. Their pizza, thick and soft as cake, is bought for reheating at home. There's a small selection of Greek cheese, coffee, jam and honey. Do not overlook the rich, moist baklava oozing with honey.

Italian

Boulangerie Corona
6901 Bordeaux Street
Montreal H2G 2S3
728-0401

This nondescript little bakery near St. Hubert and Beaubien is supplier of bread to Anjou-Québec and its very particular owner, Paris-born Maurice Pastrie. The bread is good . . . watch it come out of huge ovens at the back of the store — the same ovens that the Monaco family has been stoking since 1932. No one can explain why or how their crusty, typically Italian *chinois* and *zulu* breads got their names. Flat slabs of pizza are also a specialty here.

Boulangerie Roma
6776 St. Laurent Boulevard
Montreal H2S 3C7
273-9357

A very simple little shop just a stone's throw from Milano Fruiterie. But it hides a few real treasures. Lusty Italian bread. Creamy, homemade pistachio ice cream flecked with nuts. And a sort of *tuile*, a divine almond-based cookie rolled into tongue-shaped curls and called, *lingue di scuchera*, "sister-in-law tongues." How unkind, but how expressive!

Boulangerie-Charcuterie N.D.G.
5801 Upper Lachine Road
N.D.G. H4A 2B6
481-4215

That tiny outpost of Little Italy on the
Upper Lachine Road just west of
Décarie supports a few good Italian
bakeries and groceries. This friendly
shop is always busy with neighbors
picking up fresh bread. A good bet is
the whole-wheats. Fine selection of
Italian charcuterie, cheeses, biscotti
and olives. Baked Alaska is available
on notice.

Boulangerie & Pâtisserie Molisana
6547 Somerled Avenue
N.D.G. H4V 1S7
489-7038

This pleasant neighborhood
boulangerie-charcuterie is a good
source for homemade, fix-it-up-at-
home meals. Fresh pasta . . . golden
coronas — round loaves with a hole in
the middle . . . pizza bread — a bready
square of pizza dough for you to
decorate. A fennel-studded flatbread
which is interesting and different.

Fruit pies are made from scratch here
from seasonal fruits. Do not leave
without some *tarallucci* — lemon-
custard biscuits — a specialty of the
province of Molisana. The Matteo
family will look after you very well
indeed.

Motta Bakery and Pastry
303 Mozart Avenue East
Montreal H2S 1B8
270-5952

A gaily colored storefront brightens
Mozart Avenue at the edge of the Jean
Talon Market. Owned by the large
Crispino family, Motta gives pride of
place to homemade, marinated salads
. . . giant jars contain eggplant, mixed
vegetables, mushrooms and bean
salads. There is an enticing selection of
Italian breads and pizzas of various
shape. The specialty bread is *pane di
grano*, a crusty corn bread. Huge

takeout trays of memorable lasagna. Exit with a slice of pizza bread stuffed with spinach and ham. Devour immediately.

Old Country Bakery
8870 Verville Street
Montreal H2N 1X9
381-7181

If you know anyone who buys bread only from supermarkets – white, sliced and bagged – take him here. Old Country Bakery will bring back warm memories of going with grandmother to a "real" bakery. This nondescript, ramshackle shop slowly reveals its treasures. On first impression, a neighborhood dépanneur – where's the bread?

You'll meet customers, arms laden with bread, rolls, pizza – hands holding wonderful, lusty sandwiches on crisp, fat rolls, but where's the bread? At the very back of the store, through an opening in the wall, step down, turn right. Alice Through the Looking Glass. A huge, old-fashioned bakery with racks of cooling breads, pizzas, rolls. Choose a *corona* or *pangot* from the racks. Pile up a few pizzas for the freezer.

Old Country is located on the part of Verville north of the Métropolitain. Take a child.

Pasticceria Alati-Caserta
277 Dante Street
Montreal H2S 1K3
271-3013

An old-time Italian pastry shop on Dante Street, behind the Jean Talon Market. The Calderone family specializes in pastries and ice creams from their native Napoli. Not to be missed – their *zuppa inglese*, a custard-filled, liqueur-soaked cake – the pride of the house. Also *sfogliatelle* – a Neapolitan fan-shaped pastry filled with custard and dried fruits. *Torta al mandorla*, a traditional almond cake. Easter finds the shop crowded with flocks of delicate, white marzipan lambs. "Watermelon" slices are beautifully fashioned from marzipan. Homemade spumone, a Neapolitan ice cream, is a specialty here. Dozens of biscotti to dip in your espresso.

Pasticceria San Marco
1581 Jean Talon East
Montreal H2E 1S9
727-5401

The Buonamici family has been baking for their lucky neighborhood in Ville St. Michel for 27 years. Their crowded, friendly shop, with its one table for espresso, is packed with delicacies. The *tiramisù* cake alone is worth a trip from downtown. *Tiramisù* is an Italian trifle made with Mascarpone, a triple cream, fresh cheese. Call ahead to reserve.

The Buonamicis make their own tartufo . . . no little pre-packaged ice cream balls here. Also homemade gelati . . . the specialty flavor is whipped cream with almonds and fruit. Honey-colored *roccante* — sticky almond clusters. To dip in your wine . . . *taralli*, a biscuit made from pepper, white wine, flour and studded with fennel seeds. Wonderful meringues called *sospiri*, or "sighs."

While in the area, stop in at Pâtes Coloccia (1880 Jean Talon East) for fresh egg pasta of every description.

Peter Sowa and helper prepare Polish delicacies at Pâtisserie & Charcuterie Polonaise Wawel.

Pâtisserie & Boulangerie Italia
5540 Jean Talon East
Montreal H1S 1L9
259-0746

A bustling neighborhood bakery on an interesting stretch of Jean Talon East. Wonderfully shaped crusty breads — round, long, braided, shaped like animals. Homemade gelati. Tempting pastries — plump cannoli stuffed with sweet custard. Fresh pasta. A large collection of Italian brandied fruits in rococo bottles.

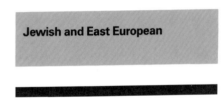

Jewish and East European

The Bagel Place
Faubourg St. Catherine
1616 St. Catherine Street West
Montreal H3H 1L7
931-2827

Isak Schneider says he's the "movie star of the Faubourg." And he's right. Hundreds of people press their nose to his window to watch him do his magic — turn simple flour, water and eggs into bagels. One can't be sure about the eggs, however, as Isak refuses to divulge his recipe. Even his staff never quite knows the exact measurements. Tom, Isak's son, a recent law school graduate, safeguards the family secret for the next generation.

Isak came from the ruins of Poland, thirty-five years ago, and began baking bagels at the St. Lawrence Bagel Bakery and then at the university of bagel baking, the Fairmount Bagel Factory. Isak figures that there are at least ten bagel bakers in the city and each one produces a unique bagel — a function of recipe, oven and wood. He is sure his are the best. And who can argue with a man who produces and sells forty dozen bagels an hour — onion, sesame, garlic, caraway, pumpernickel, cinnamon-raisin?

What does Isak eat for breakfast? A cinnamon-raisin bagel with cream cheese and lox. Sounds good.

Boulangerie Alex Ropeleski et Fils
2195 Gascon Avenue
Montreal H2K 2W3
522-5153

The Gascon Avenue - Ontario Street area was home to generations of Polish immigrants. One can see the remnants of poet Louis Dudek's neighborhood in the occasional Polish deli or grocery. Enter Alex Ropeleski's bakery through the simple, worn red door and enter another time and place. A wonderful, old-fashioned bakery with wooden floors and brick ovens.

Bakers work steps away from their customers, kneading and slamming dough into greased molds and carrying worn wooden trays off to rise into mounds of eggy challah or babka. Customers choose their breads directly

from the cooling racks. Exotic Polish names — *zytni, razowy, pleciona* — translate into the familiar rye, cracked wheat and egg loaf twist.

The sons of Alex Ropeleski have sold the bakery to the Marshals, who have promised to uphold the Polish traditions and recipes. Mme Marshal, a French-Canadian, has won the respect of her clientele by learning a passable Polish. And M. Marshal, a master pastry chef trained in his native Alsace, has become adept at Polish bread-making.

Henry, one of the Ropeleski sons, often visits the bakery to lend technical advice and a helping hand. A customer of Polish origin told the story of Henry, who literally wore out his hips and knee bones pounding up the three-storey, outdoor staircases that define this part of Montreal. The customer had not forgotten that Ropeleski's Bakery had fed the Polish community during the Great Depression. Loyal customers are forever grateful. Bread with a history.

Boulangerie Boyman
4874 St. Laurent Boulevard
Montreal H2T 1R5
845-5713

Boyman's is part theater, part bakery. A good place to meet real "main streeters." An old-fashioned wholesale and retail bakery specializing in East European-style breads — crispy ryes, mahogany Russians, wonderful, eggy challahs. Enormous ovens that never shut down. Watch the bakers haul trays and trays of bread from ovens to racks. A good place to bring children. The best price in town on bagels. Boyman's slicing machines belong in the Smithsonian. Get here before this part of St. Laurent falls to the yuppies.

Pâtisserie Toman
1421 Mackay Street
Montreal H3G 2H6
844-1605

Founded by Miroslav Toman, owner of a renowned pastry shop in Prague, this charming, well-worn café-bakery could be grandmother's kitchen on baking day. Toman, a well-known pastry chef in Czechoslovakia, was a legendary figure among Czech émigrés. He is remembered as much for destroying all his bakery equipment before fleeing the Communist takeover of his homeland as for his pastries. As soon as Toman opened his store in Montreal, he had a following of loyal Czech émigrés. Toman sold the café several years ago to Robert Potuzil, who has continued to make Toman's specialties.

Climb the stairs of the old gray-stone house on Mackay. Thimble-sized tarts for tea . . . luscious chocolate tarts doused in Grand Marnier . . . raspberry tarts soaked in slivovitz. Fat apple strudel waits to be asked home. Choose from Vienna crescents dusted with sugar, dense, chocolaty mousse cakes or truffles oozing with liqueur. Hearty soups are made each day for takeout. With prior notice, master cake builder Potuzil can create a wedding or birthday cake that will dazzle your guests.

Pâtisserie & Charcuterie Polonaise Wawel
2524 Ontario Street East
Montreal H2K 1W4
524-3348

Peter Sowa is one of those happy Canadian immigrant stories. Peter, now 26, came to Canada five years ago from Kalisz, Poland. Canada Manpower told him that this country needed bakers. A baker he became. He rented a small corner in the back of an Italian bakery on St. Dominique and sold his *paczki*, Polish doughnuts, by word of mouth, through the immigrant community. Soon he was able to open his own shop. Wawel, named after the royal palace of Krakow, is a homey, simple shop which attracts Polish, Ukrainian and German customers from all over Montreal.

Golden, sugar-dusted kugelhupf

Wawel's star attraction is babka —
a bread-like coffee cake dotted with
raisins and lightly glazed with rum.
A gingerbread like no other . . . giant
slabs slathered with Swedish cream
and thick plum butter. Two kinds of
cheesecake . . . one for the Viennese,
high and delicate. The other . . . in the
style of Krakow . . . raisins, a sugar
dough base and a lattice-work top.
There's golden kugelhupf, and crispy,
delicate *faworki*, an airy cookie fried in
oil and dusted with sugar — the second
cousin of the Jewish *kuchel*. Poppy
seed strudel, walnut cakes, vanilla
babkas.

Peter's customers know to ask for
pierogis and *uszka*, which are hidden
in the back. *Pierogis* — dumplings that
come stuffed three ways — either with

beef, or sauerkraut and mushrooms, or
cheese and potatoes. *Uszka* are even
smaller dumplings to be added to
borsch.

Wawel is an informal Polish community
center. Although the community has
migrated to the west of the island, true
believers return to Wawel for a taste of
the old country.

Renfell Baking and Cooking
5331 Décarie Boulevard
Snowdon H3W 3C4
489-9488

Just down the street from the
Snowdon Deli, Morris Renfell bakes
one of the best challahs in town. Great
mounds of eggy, raisin-filled "special
challahs" for Jewish festivals. And of
course, on order, extra-long challahs
for festive occasions. Crusty pumper-
nickels and ryes adorn the shelves.
Light and airy *kuchel* — fried dough
confections — are wonderful for tea
dunking. There are heavy little knishes
bursting with buckwheat or potato.
Kosher-style egg rolls and pizza rolls.

Chocolate or cinnamon Danish that are
positively habit forming. Crunchy
poppy seed cookies and almondy
mandelbrodt must not be overlooked.
Three-cornered *hamantashen*, named
after the wicked Haman, are sweet,
sticky and filling.

Sticky pistachio-studded baklava

Renfell makes a memorable Roumanian strudel — a luscious dessert strudel with a crackling crust and a treasure of raisins and Turkish delight. A tiny hole-in-the-wall store usually identified by the Mercedes and BMW's double-parked outside.

St. Lawrence Bakery
3830 St. Laurent Boulevard
Montreal H2W 1X6
845-4536

An institution on the Main. Don't let the fluorescent lighting turn you off — or the East European salesladies capable of throwing a man across a wrestling ring. Crusty Jewish and Mittel European breads are the only decoration here. Venture in and find huge slabs of cheesecake baked in trencher-long pans . . . buy it by the piece or the kilo. Huge *hamantashen*, triangular-shaped cookies hiding prune or poppy seed filling. Crackling crisp *kuchel* and plump raisin breads are among the staggering number of breads baked here. If you're looking for a meter-long braided challah for a celebration, this is where you can get it, but order a few days in advance.

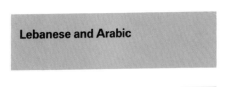

Lebanese and Arabic

Pâtisserie Armenia
355 Henri Bourassa West
Montreal H3L 1N9
366-1471

There is a considerable Armenian and Lebanese community in the neighborhoods at the edge of the back river, where the end of St. Denis Street meets Gouin Boulevard. Verdant, well-kept properties border on busy Henri Bourassa. Proprietor K. H. Merdjanian came to Montreal from Erevan, now in Soviet Armenia. This is a very simple, little shop and the counters may look bare, but have no fear, simply ask for the items that are listed on the board and they will appear.

There's *chiche barak* — an Armenian ravioli stuffed with chickpeas. Puffy, golden, cheese-filled turnovers. Salted breadsticks. And Arab bread stuffed with tahina (sesame paste). The specialty here is *lahmadjoun*, the Armenian "pizza," slathered with chopped beef and onions. Thick, homemade yogurt is made here . . . so different from supermarket yogurt.

Pâtisserie Atlas
1051 Bernard Avenue West
Outremont H2V 1V1
274-8685

Even if a stroll along Bernard Avenue weren't so pleasant, the *madkassh*, Armenian bread, from Atlas would lure me there. Sonia and Artin have been baking here for eight years. Sonia will gladly guide you through the mysteries of her oriental delicacies — *kaymak*, for instance, a heavenly cream taken as dessert with a dollop of honey, or, better still, date syrup. *Kaymak* is a close cousin to English clotted cream. Atlas makes a variety of honey-doused pastries based on phyllo dough. Longtime Atlas customers always pick up a pound or two of homemade Turkish delight . . . and you should, too.

Pâtisserie Dorée
1560 Dudemaine Street
Cartierville H3M 1R2
331-3232

Across the street from Restaurant Zahle, Pâtisserie Dorée specializes in Syrian pastries. Nadim Mahrousé, the brother of Nazem of Liège Street's elegant Pâtisserie Mahrousé, is a friendly, mustachioed baker. He is enormously proud, and justly so, of his baked treasures. Heavy trays of sausage-shaped baklava stuffed with pistachios sit on counters surrounded by bags of sugared almonds. Try

Syrian-style Turkish delight — full of pistachios but without the customary dusting of powdered sugar. Do not leave without a dozen coconut macaroons — astonishingly buttery, although made without butter. Bliss.

Pâtisserie Mahrousé
1010 Liège Street West
Town of Mount Royal H3N 1B8
279-1629

Hiding in the shadow of the mammoth Rockland Shopping Center is a little working-class street called Liège. Paris is full of such streets — dull and gray, but hiding a jewel. The jewel of Liège is Pâtisserie Mahrousé, a sophisticated shop on a street of dépanneurs. Look for the distinctive maroon awning with Arabic inscription. The shop's clientele is mostly Armenians who have emigrated from Arab countries, Syrians and Lebanese. An Arabic sign behind the counter exhorts those far from their homeland to remain faithful to the place of their birth.

Trays and trays of cakes and sweets line the sparkling pink counters beckoning like some fantasy of Scheherazade. Sticky baklava with poetic names.. *sawr*, ''a bracelet'' . . . *kol shokor*, ''eat and praise the Lord'' . . . lush rich *chaubert*, a puff pastry confection filled with cream, available only on the weekend. Marzipan molded into perfect fruit shapes. Fat little apricots dipped in milk chocolate.

Syrian-born Nazem Mahrousé and his staff prepare dozens of dainty packets of spinach or cheese triangles for hors d'oeuvres. Kibbe, a chopped lamb and bulgur patty, and finger-sized dolmas – vine leaves stuffed with rice and raisins – are also offered as hors d'oeuvres. *Halloune*, a creamy white cheese, to be served with date syrup, makes a luscious dessert.

A shopping expedition to Rockland should always include a stop at Pâtisserie Mahrousé – although Pâtisserie Mahrousé is worth a trip on its own merit.

Fantasies of Scheherazade at Pâtisserie Mahrousé

South American

Boulangerie El Refugio Panderia
4648 St. Laurent Boulevard
Montreal H2T 1R3
845-1358

A meeting place for the city's growing Chilean population. Beef empanadas – crisp pastry turnovers filled with minced beef – are always available. Chicken, seafood, or cheese empanadas can be ordered with advance notice. South American-style bread – *allulla*, round shaped – *colisa*, a square-shaped roll – are baked throughout the day. The "Berlin," a popular doughnut brought to South America by early German immigrants, is soft, doughy and comforting.

El Reencuentro/La Rencontre
5201 St. Urbain Street
Montreal H2T 2W8
270-7369

A lively corner cafe with lusty takeout fare. Empanadas to go. Also *churassco* – a spicy steak sandwich – smothered with tomatoes and soft, buttery avocados. *Barros luco*, a variation of *churassco*, with the addition of a melt of cheese. Watch the bakers prepare the distinctive bread used for sandwiches. Repress that Big Mac attack and reach for a *churassco*.

Butcher Shops and Delicatessens

Montreal's small service-oriented butcher shops are a ready antidote to the anonymous pre-packaged, pre-cut wastelands of supermarket meat counters. The confidence engendered by a friendly, knowledgeable butcher can often compensate for the slightly higher prices one pays. The range of nationalities, the breadth of specialties are once again a tribute to Montreal's ethnic stew. Are there that many cities that can boast of a profusion of French, Halal, kosher or South American butchers?

Eighty years young, Sam Seltzer still loves serving "his" ladies at N.D.G. Meat Market.

Canadian

N.D.G. Meat Market
5343 Sherbrooke Street West
Montreal H4A 1Z4
489-8621

Faubourg St. Catherine
1616 St. Catherine Street West
Montreal H3H 1L7
935-6129

Sam Seltzer started N.D.G. Meat Market fifty-eight years ago and it still stands in its original spot. Sam says that he's over ''seventy years old plus his bar mitzvah.'' His two sons, Norman and Nelson, can't get him to slow down. Sam's behind the counter most days doing what he likes best: serving, charming his ''ladies'' and cutting meat.

Sam has conveyed his love of the business to his two sons. Norman began working for his father when he was eleven. Norman is a keen observer of the marketplace. He understands women. ''A woman doesn't like to wait too long. A woman likes attention from her butcher. Every woman is treated like a queen here. She's recognized here. And if she's coming to buy meat from me, I want her recognized.'' It's this philosophy and the superior quality of the N.D.G. product that have spelled success for the Seltzers.

Fifty-five employees of every nationality staff the mother store on Sherbrooke Street. Second-floor cutting rooms are beehives of activity. Carcasses are cut down and trimmed. A hamburger machine stamps out patties by the hundreds. Kidneys are weighed and bagged. Boxes are carted into the cooler and out.

The Sherbrooke Street operation supplies some of the best restaurants and steak houses in Montreal, as well as its own outlet at the Faubourg St. Catherine. Each employee has a special role to play in the enormous organized confusion of this busy meat market. Norman praises his staff,

In the cold room, cutting down carcasses

throwing the success of N.D.G. to their shoulders. "Can a business run with one person? Not really. Everybody counts here. My father. My brother. Me. My butchers. And even my floor washer, who's very important to us." One key employee is Terry Jacobs, who for the last seventeen years has been the telephone voice of N.D.G., making sure that the steaks, briskets, racks of lamb are delivered to the right houses on time.

The Seltzer brothers choose their own beef carcasses from the slaughterhouses, looking for young meat with a good marbling and covering of fat. "I don't want frozen. I don't want Cryovac." Beef carcasses are then aged anywhere from twenty-one to twenty-eight days. The Seltzers insist on Provimi veal from specially fed calves, for a "nice, creamy white-pink" meat. Lamb comes from New Zealand or a supplier in Alberta. Norman says he "smokes his own turkeys and chickens. And I make my own salami. The way it should be made."

N.D.G. is known for its steaks and beef roasts and especially for what Norman calls "the king of all roasts — prime rib." He says that he loves "a rib . . . 'cause it's got the marbling, it's got the bone, it's got everything." Some customers swear by N.D.G.'s skirt steaks, others by the veal briskets. The corned beef brisket is unique and the wonderful "lollipop" steaks, whose origins are lost to memory, are surely the signature of N.D.G.

Shop early in the day. Get to know Terry on the phone. Make yourself known to Sam, Norman and Nelson and you'll be a star at N.D.G.

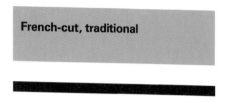

French-cut, traditional

Anjou-Québec
1025 Laurier Avenue West
Outremont H2V 2L1
272-4065

Anjou-Québec is the "grand-père" of the traditional French butcher shop in Montreal . . . and there are very few that still exist in the city. Dozens of young butchers from France have trained at the side of Paris-born Maurice Pastrie since 1953. French butchering is substantially different from the North American style. The cuts are leaner and more tender because each cut is taken from one muscle. The standard Canadian cut across several muscles results in a tougher cut.

Meat counters at Anjou-Québec are artfully arranged — like jewels in a shop window. Butchers, in impossibly white, starched coats work alongside M. Pastrie to fill the counters with bavette, filet mignon, dainty packages of paupiettes stuffed with minced veal, razor-thin slices of beef fondue and other specialties of the French cut.

There is a limited, but extremely well-edited selection of fruits and vegetables jammed into the free spaces around the counters . . . thin, thin green beans hours from Rungis, tender shoots of mâche – lamb's lettuce – perfect tomatoes. The cheese counter waves the French flag . . . as M. Pastrie cultivates a select collection from La Belle France.

Trimming a buttery side of Scotch salmon at Anjou

Alas, Paris is too far away, or the pastries would arrive from Dalloyau and the bread from Poilâne. Here the pastries are ordered from Pâtisserie de Gascogne and the bread from La Gerbe d'Or and Boulangerie Corona. The freezer section boasts colorfully labeled microwave containers of *coq au vin*, *lapin chasseur* – the traditional dishes of a good bourgeois kitchen. Look for Pâtisserie de Gascogne's outstanding sorbets and ice creams.

Anjou-Québec is the closest one can get in Montreal to the true boucherie française, and Maurice Pastrie, with his snow-white coat, his impeccable manners and his wondrous mustache, is surely a master of his art.

Boucherie des Ardennes
5010 De Salaberry Street
Cartierville H4J 1H9
331-7010

The north end of the city, not far from Pâtisserie de Gascogne, is home to Daniel Ducay's French butcher shop – another training ground for young butchers from France. Counters brim with the traditional French cuts: well-trimmed bavettes, dainty noisettes of lamb, croquettes – patties of minced veal, breaded and waiting to be sautéed – homemade, garlicky *saucisson de Lyon* and *andouillette*, a small tripe sausage.

The prepared meals at Ardennes are classic – an exquisite filet of beef Wellington, for instance, frozen in portions for one. Homey *cassoulet*. Tiny *escargots en brioche*. Combine this stop with a pilgrimage to Pâtisserie de Gasgogne.

Boucherie Chevaline France Canada
1142 Van Horne Avenue
Montreal H2V 1J8
277-7788

A very fussy French butcher introduced me to this shop — a tidy, clean place selling, well, horse meat. Somehow, filet of horse sounds better in French. *Filet de cheval* was on special the day I visited. Also rabbits, hare and grain-fed chicken. Rabbit stuffed with green peppers and roast pork with prunes are specialties of the house.

Boucherie Française de Lyon
6111 Monkland Avenue
N.D.G. H4A 1H5
481-7576

While shopping on Monkland, drop in at this friendly store for a Marcelino bread. A marvelous crusty baguette, made by an Italian baker in St. Thérèse, it's the closest cousin to a proper Parisian baguette this side of the Atlantic. M. Benitou of Lyon is a rosy-faced butcher who does a beautiful crown roast of lamb and makes all his own sausages, as he would if he were back in Lyon.

Boucherie de France
730 Décarie Boulevard
St. Laurent H4L 3L5
744-5116

In the heart of St. Laurent's Décarie shopping area, this shop carries a constant, consistent supply of game meat. Bustling Mme Martinelli, formerly of Marseille, will supply Alberta bison in steaks or tournedos, wild boar and, in mid-April of each year, caribou. There are homemade pâtés of game, pheasant and rabbit. Marcelino bread.

Le Maître Boucher
5686 Monkland Avenue
N.D.G. H4A 1E4
487-1437

Herman Lévesque, *le maître boucher*, is a young, obliging neighborhood butcher. Customers are welcomed to his shop and, in the words of one of his customers, "enveloped in his warmth." Lévesque's meat is very good. There are his specialties — fresh game, New Zealand venison, grain-fed chicken and a surprise, seafood sausages. Look for fresh chicken breasts "cordon bleu" and *paupiettes de veau* stuffed with apricots and minced veal, artfully tied like little presents. *Cretons maison* and *galantine de volaille* are well made. Hard-to-find veal and fish stock are found in the freezer. The store bread is a healthy French loaf made with white flour and bran. Lévesque makes you feel as if you were his most important customer.

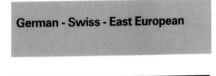

German - Swiss - East European

Les Aliments Felix Mish
1903 Jolicoeur Street
Ville Émard H4E 1X4
766-2094

Les Aliments Felix Mish first opened thirty-five years ago in the old Polish district around Ontario and Rouen Streets. Now located on the border

Strawberry festival at Le Maître Boucher

of Ville Émard and Côte St. Paul, it attracts Polish-Canadians from all over the city for old country specialties — sausages smoked for hours over maple, smoked meat, bacon, head-cheese, kielbasa and kishka, a sausage made from buckwheat and blood. Check the freezer for ready-to-cook *pierogi*, or little dumplings, and for *bigos*, a sauerkraut and meat dish — the national dish of Poland. Ropeleski breads and Wawel pastries are delivered to the store several times a week from the old Polish district.

Ronnie Mish runs the business since the death of his father, Felix. Not much has changed and not much will. Solid, ancient machinery — a sausage stuffer, a meat chopper — is impeccably shined, cleaned and in use to this day. The recipes have not varied since Felix came from Poland and opened his shop door. ''And why should they?'' says Ronnie.

Alpina Market
3885 Perron Boulevard
Chomedey H7V 1P8
681-6860

The outlet store for the Alpina Salami Company, Alpina is owned by the Piacek family who came to Canada from the Slovak side of Czechoslovakia. There's a tremendous range of salamis and sausages available here . . . from Slovak salami to Dutch sausage. The list seems endless and fascinating — chorizo, Hungarian salami, Swiss salami, teewurst, Krakowsa, cabanos, szogedi, kielbasa — sometimes only the all-important spicing changes the nationality of a salami. There's a diet ham that has "almost no salt," says Frau Piacek, quite carefully underlining the "almost."

The German Krauter brand of teas is carried here . . . difficult to find, difficult to love, varieties such as mistletoe, hawthorn, wormwood and nettle. An exhaustive collection of the Dr. Oetker baking products line. German-language periodicals available.

European Sausage
1746 Richardson Street
Point St. Charles H3K 1G5
932-4545

Once you find this factory store, you will be hooked. European is a secret shared by thousands of smart Montrealers. Just over the Lachine Canal on an industrial street sandwiched between St. Patrick and Central. Well worth the search. Freshly produced sausages, well-aged hams and salami are treated with due reverence by the knowledgeable staff. Irene speaks five languages and knows her product.

European Sausage is a culinary shrine for the city's Ukrainian and East European population. Kielbasa, a garlicky Ukrainian-Polish sausage, and Krakowsa, a ham salami, are big sellers here. Other Slavic treats are "flat"

bacon, more meaty than ordinary bacon and a cooked, rolled bacon studded with peppercorns. There's a popular "smoked meat" meat loaf, gypsy ham and all manner of East European sausage. The *varenikes* are a must — small dumplings filled with sauerkraut or potato.

Smoked turkeys and chickens available on a week's notice. Kasha and poppy seeds by the sack. Christmas and Easter the store is jammed with Ukrainian holiday specialties. European is a stop for people who weekend at points south. Minutes from the Champlain and Victoria bridges.

Hoffner Salaison Boucherie
3671 St. Laurent Boulevard
Montreal H2X 2V5
845-9809

An important outpost of the Austro-Hungarian Empire and local evidence that pork products in the form of ham, bacon and sausage play an important part in Middle European cuisine. European dried mushrooms are given pride of place here. Hoffner's carries a large variety of packaged Swiss and Austrian breads, as well as Oblaten, thin biscuit wafers used in cake-making. You'll find bitters, Balkan jams and armies of people devouring sausages from the shop grill.

Salamico

1980 Place Thimens
St. Laurent H4R 1L1
336-8711

Well known to Montreal's German and Swiss community, Salamico's factory store is one of the best meat stores in the city. White-tiled walls and red-tiled floors seem just the right setting for the thirty-foot-long meat counter. The specialties here are French-cut meats and Salamico's own sausages, salamis and hams. German specialties predominate — rouladen, debreziner, wienerwurst, teewurst, schaufele, smoked tongue. Sauerbraten, marinated beef, is available year-round, while marinated steaks are a summer feature.

Regulars know to arrive on Fridays and Saturdays when hot specialties like meat loaf or roast pork stuffed with a coarse meat loaf are pulled steaming from the oven. Cold-cut platters for parties must be ordered in advance. German specialty groceries such as Bahlsen biscuits and Sarotti chocolates predominate. Also German- and Swiss-style breads from local bakeries, both fresh and packaged. A nice, friendly place . . . gemütlichkeit prevails.

Slovenia Meat Market

3653 St. Laurent Boulevard
Montreal H2X 2V5
842-3558

A wonderland of East European smoked meats and sausages . . . paprika-dusted bacons, mounds of knockwurst, bratwurst and kielbasa. Mittel European definitely spoken here. Don't trip over the buckets of pickled whole cabbages and sauerkraut. Still lifes of Hungarian and Yugoslav jarred and marinated salads. Poppy seed strudel adorns the countertops and sausages hang from every possible inch of ceiling. Only amazing willpower and inner strength will allow you to walk past the steaming grill of

Miklos Foldes of Favorite Viande displays sepia photographs of a Hungarian childhood.

sausages, *prêt-à-manger*, without
trying one or two — with sauerkraut.

Favorite Viande et Charcuterie
5675 Monkland Avenue
N.D.G. H4A 1E5
482-1933

When Miklos Foldes came from
Hungary twenty-eight years ago, he
had already been a master butcher for
years. He proudly shows his visitor
evocative, sepia photographs of his
childhood in Hungary . . . a smiling
Miklos, at thirteen, in a row of white-
aproned apprentice butchers, knives in
hand.

A tidy, tiny black and white tiled taste
of old Hungary, Favorite is a meeting
place for expatriate Hungarians.
They come for the old country pork
specialties central to the cuisine:
kocsonya, pork in jelly — or *kolbas*, a
pork sausage accented with garlic,
paprika and cloves — or *gyulae*, a dried
sausage. Sausage-making is an
honored skill in Hungary and
Hungarians in Montreal pay homage
to Foldes.

Mr. Foldes proudly displays his
extensive selection of foie gras, so
important to prosperous Mittel
Europeans and makes sure the visitor
tastes the homemade *korozot*, a
sheep's milk cheese spread seasoned
with paprika and studded with
caraway. Holiday time sees packs
of gaily wrapped Easter bunnies or
squadrons of red-coated Santas march

across the counters. There's a good
selection of German, Yugoslavian and
Hungarian canned goods.

The specialty here, says Foldes, is
service — and several customers nod
their heads in agreement.

Greek

Salaison P.X. Packers
696 Jean Talon West
Montreal H3N 1R8
279-4870

The window is a shocker, but then
again this is a serious butcher shop.
Fresh-killed goats, pigs and lamb,
complete with hair, hang by their tails
in the front display windows. Tommy,
the butcher, explains that hanging the
animals, skin on, for 24 hours, assures
that the meat remains tender, white
and clean. He buys only Quebec-bred
animals from breeders he trusts.

This is the place to come for a lamb or
piglet for a spit barbecue. Another
barbecue specialty is *kororetsi* — a
delicacy made by stuffing the internal
stomach lining of a lamb with the
lungs, liver and sweetbreads of the
animal. *Kororetsi* is roasted on a spit
and sliced like souvlaki. Enormous
butcher blocks with lots of history and
a sheepskin impaled to the wall are the
only decoration.

International

South American

Boucherie St. Laurent
3785 St. Laurent Boulevard
Montreal H2W 1X8
845-0186

Should you require a pig's head, stop
here. It certainly stopped me. The pig's
head glaring at me from the counter
won my immediate attention. Feet, tails,
ears also available. This busy market
around the corner from Waldman's has
hard-to-find caul fat and casings for
sausage-making. Friendly butchers
will prepare freezer orders on notice.

St. Viateur Meat Market
118 St. Viateur Street West
Montreal H2T 2L1
276-6759

A simple butcher shop, one of those
wonderful ethnic complexities so
typical of Montreal, run for the last 24
years by an Italian, who prepares
South American cuts for the neighborhood's growing Latin community.
Salvadorans, Chileans, Uruguayans
stop in for Argentine sausage,
chinchulines (sweetbreads) and salt
cod.

Poultry

Zinman Poultry
7022 St. Dominique Street
Montreal H2S 3B7
277-4302

Combine a trip to the Jean Talon
Market with one to Zinman's. Not quite
the poultry store Grandma went to – but
almost. The butcher at Zinman's will
catch you a live pigeon, pheasant, rabbit
or turkey from the pens and slaughter
it for you. You'll know it's fresh. Farm
eggs available by the dozens.

Fish Stores

We've been blessed with one of the all-time, world-class fish markets. Waldman's has served Montreal now for decades . . . through the times when we didn't know a hake from a tuna fish. It deserves enormous credit for introducing Montreal to fish and shellfish varieties from around the world. We're eating more fish today and we are more demanding about quality and freshness. Sushi bars have opened up another dimension in the enjoyment of fish. The profusion of Greek restaurants which prepare the freshest of fish over the grill has also established fish in our diets. It's now possible to buy doctor fish, blue line fish, Norwegian gravlax and fresh sardines.

Pêcheries Atlantiques du Québec
787 du Marché Central Street
Montreal H4N 1J8
382-9070

Leave some room in the car after a visit to Épicerie En Gros Métropolitaine. Pêcheries Atlantiques is just across the parking lot of the Central Market, the sprawling wholesale fruit and vegetable market north of the Métropolitain. Specialists in bulk frozen seafood, suppliers to hotels, restaurants and institutions, Pêcheries Atlantiques welcomes the retail customer. Many items are packaged for the small household. Good prices on smoked salmon, lobster and frozen shellfish.

Poissonnerie Algarve
4375 St. Laurent Boulevard
Montreal H2W 1Z8
849-5416

Combine a trip to Samos Bakery with a stop at this neighboring fishmonger. Algarve's counters are packed with iced and gleaming fish, as fresh as a Greek cook could want. There's also a large variety of dried fish. Pots of glistening Greek olives and colorful canisters of golden home country olive oil adorn the windows.

Poissonnerie Océan Fraîche
1430 St. Louis Street
St. Laurent H4L 2P3
747-7180

Just off Décarie Boulevard in St. Laurent, this is a clean blue and white tiled fish warehouse. Primarily serving the restaurant trade, its friendly staff welcomes the retail customer. A good place to pick up bulk frozen seafood products at reasonable prices.

La Reine de la Mer
1840 Dorchester Boulevard East
Montreal H2X 4P1
522-6703

La Reine de la Mer is impressive. A sparkling, clean, blue and white tiled shop attached to La Reine de la Mer Restaurant. Large portholed windows throw sunlight on counters of fish absolutely glowing with freshness. No fishy smells here. Kosta Katsoulis has been a fishmonger for thirty years. La Reine may not carry the variety of Waldman's, but product quality is unsurpassed.

Counters of baby shark, red snapper, porgy and grouper glisten in chips of ice. Also newcomers from Hawaii — blue line snapper, angel fish and doctor fish. Fresh, not frozen, halibut. La Reine supplies sushi bars with fresh tuna, Portuguese rascas and scorpene.

Store manager Raymond Sansregret says that fishmen have a saying, "Follow the Japanese and they will take you to the fresh fish."

There are ten lobster tanks. Fifty counter feet of frozen seafood . . . an interesting "crown" of frozen cooked shrimp surrounding seafood sauce — thaw and serve. Not to be missed: frozen packages of marinated salmon from Norway — subtly smoked and flecked with dill. Pale pink slabs of Arctic char. Well-chosen smoked fish and select caviar.

A friendly, well-informed staff, ready with recipes and advice. Very well organized . . . choose your product,

have it weighed and priced at the weighing station, pass through the cash, hand it to the men in the glass-enclosed room and watch them scale and clean your catch. Ample parking. Open seven days a week.

The Smokehouse
4444 Coloniale Avenue
Montreal H2W 2C7
844-0240

The Smokehouse deserves landmark status. The Coloniale Avenue neighborhood is infused with a sweet, honeyed smell. The old brick building hides an extraordinary occupation for a dense downtown area. The Smokehouse earns its name smoking

Fishing at La Reine de la Mer

fish for stores and for the fishermen who bring in their catch. Huge vats jammed with floating salmon filets or whitefish or carp. The sweet smell is revealed: the salmon is bathed in water, salt and brown sugar, giving the air a candied flavor.

Ettore Redo, who manages the operation for Levitt's Kosher Foods, carefully loads the smoker with just the right mixture of excelsior and sawdust to produce a precise blend of fragrance and smoke. Buy a side of salmon from Ettore or bring your own fish to be smoked.

The Smokehouse is strictly kosher and will accept for smoking only those fish that have scales. Ettore will smoke any fish for $13 — large or small. All fish are created equal here. It's a bit like dry-cleaning . . . pick it up in eight days.

Ettore Redo and a rack of freshly smoked whitefish

Groceries

I am convinced that if one looks long enough and hard enough all manner of edible things can be found in Montreal – from palm nut soup to dried persimmons. Each new wave of immigration has left Montreal a more interesting place to shop for food. The Chinese have created a vibrant shopping area on St. Laurent and de La Gauchetière. The City of St. Laurent is dotted with Arab and Lebanese groceries. Lower Victoria Avenue in Snowdon pulsates to the beat of reggae music and is infused with the exotic scents of curries. Montrealers, whatever their ethnic background, are becoming more familiar with new cuisines, and more interested in finding authentic ingredients.

British

Marks and Spencer
The Montreal Trust Building
1500 McGill College Avenue
Montreal H3A 3J5
499-8558

The quintessential store for British nursery and comfort foods. A craving for Melton Mowbray or Scotch pies can be satisfied here. A "Marks and Sparks" favorite is double cream — a heavenly, but fattening mortal sin to be lobbed onto strawberries. British treasures — gluey steak and kidney pie, gray minced beef and onion pasties, leaden pork and egg pies, extra-strong tea and mediocre scones. Just like England.

La Tulipe Noire Café
2100 Stanley Street
Montreal H3A 3G3
285-1225

Despite its French name, this trendy, downtown café-boutique is an anglophile's culinary heaven. The boutique handles a number of cottage industry, "gifty" food items from the British Isles. You may find Elsenham jams and preserves elsewhere, but you'll search long and hard for Isle of

Opposite: Oven warm menahis at Adonis

Arran Wild Bramble Jelly. Should you ache for Welsh, and not Welch, jams, head for La Tulipe Noire and Welsh Lady jams. The shop stocks some gastronomic esoterica . . . A craving for pineapple in syrup with crème de menthe? Look no further.

Cash and Carry

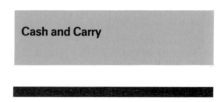

Épicerie En Gros Métropolitaine
1050 du Marché Central Street
Montreal H4N 1S8
389-8261

A sprawling "cash and carry" at Central Market . . . a boon to those with large families, a country house, an impending banquet, a nursery school or a small menagerie. This is the place where small stores do their shopping and you can too. Prices are well below retail. Shopkeepers don't pay sales tax, but the retail customer must.

Métropolitaine has a huge selection of groceries and many imported and specialty items. The shopper must buy groceries by the half case or case. Not so dairy and institutional items. This is the place to come for two kilos of cream cheese, ten gallons of ice cream, a case of bathroom tissue, tons of candy for Halloween, three kilos of hot dogs for the office party, a case of frozen orange juice. This place is fun. No kids under twelve.

Dutch

The Dutch Mill
5216 Côte des Neiges
Montreal H3T 1X8
733-2646

The Dutch Mill calls itself "the only Dutch specialty shop in Montreal." We are lucky to have one. The Dutch community has moved out to the West Island and to the South Shore. Henny Vanderdonk, a lovely lady with a charming accent, enjoys showing visitors her specialties — croquettes, minced beef rolled in bread crumbs

and ready to deep-fry, homemade pepper pâté, raw Holland herring, smoked beef and Leyden cheese with cloves.

Henny carries the proper smoked sausage for authentic Dutch pea soup and her *krente bollen* — currant balls — are sure to bring back the taste of the old country. A selection of Dutch groceries and tobacco products. Walk out in a pair of bright yellow wooden shoes.

Henny and her bright yellow wooden shoes

Filipino

Greek

Épicerie Manila
20 Roy Street East
Montreal H2W 2S6
844-8768

A lively Filipino meeting place. The
cheerful lady at the cash register is
happy to help unravel the mysteries of
coconut gel, banana sauce and *burong
mangosa*. The complex Filipino cuisine
depends on a variety of Filipino, Thai
and Japanese products. You'll find
Thai pickled eggplant as well as fresh
Japanese vegetables. Homemade
shrimp and vegetable rolls make an
exotic take-home appetizer.

Filipino videos, delicate blue and white
Japanese crockery and an intriguing
automatic rice dispenser decorate
the shelves. The shop sells colorful
embroidered Filipino soft shoes, but
that does not mean that its heart
belongs to Imelda. Cory Aquino's
biography is on prominent display
here.

Sakaris Brothers' Fruit Market
4393 St. Laurent Boulevard
Montreal H2W 1Z8
844-5143

This lively market is run by the Sakaris
family, but you won't find their name
on the sign. Look for a huge cow's
head. The produce is of very good
quality and you will find items such as
rappini, collard and dandelion leaves.
Huge barrels of salty Greek feta and
bathtubs of Greek olives glistening with
oil attract loyal customers. Hard-to-find
Greek cheeses are plentiful here. Take
home some aromatic dried herbs from
the Greek mountains for a proper
home country cure.

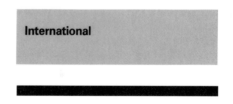

International

Super Marché Latina
11847 Lachapelle Street
St. Laurent H4J 2M1
331-5879

The Salterelli family started their
business on St. Viateur Street, where
the original store still stands at number
185. They followed their ethnic market
to the northwest of the city, settling in

St. Laurent with its large multinational
community. Today they serve a mosaic
of Lebanese, Pakistanis, Armenians,
Spaniards, Salvadorans, Italians and
Greeks.

This is a big supermarket, but no
ordinary supermarket. These grocers
pay attention to the culinary needs of
their customers. Latina is a
multicultural stew of products. Hard-
to-find *achiote* seeds for Tex-Mex
cooking, Brazilian coffee, Italian
Mascarpone, Greek oils, Lebanese
cereals, tortillas, Oriental spinach and
chorizo. A large assortment of variety
meats — beef hearts, tongues, lamb
tripe. Reasonably priced and good
vegetables.

Tony Salterelli says his customers all
have a desire to try new products,
whatever their ethnic background.
French-Canadians are crazy for falafel,
a Middle Eastern ground bean dish.

Do note: Laurentien Boulevard
becomes Lachapelle on the east side
after Henri Bourassa. A good place to
stop on your way to Pâtisserie de
Gascogne on Gouin Boulevard.

Italian

Faema
14 Jean Talon West
Montreal H2R 2W5
276-2671

A busy, homey café-groceria with a
seductive choice of made-in-front-of-
you takeout food. Mama is often at the
counter preparing exquisite, tiny
stuffed artichokes or rolling out
fettuccine from a huge pasta machine.
A trip to Milano should include a visit to
Faema . . . just to see what's cooking.
Terrific selection of Italian coffee
makers, coffee and Italian crockery.

Milano Fruiterie
6884 St. Laurent Boulevard
Montreal H2S 3C7
273-8558

Little Italy has shopped at Milano
since 1956. Redolent with cheese and
spices, jammed with oils and vinegars,
colored with firm, bright vegetables,
gaudy with foil-wrapped cakes, Milano
has, well, atmosphere.

A remarkable collection of Italian fresh
cheeses — small *bocconcini* floating in
salted water, creamy ricottas, low-fat
tuma and triple cream Mascarpone.
Real buffalo milk mozzarella will arrive
shortly. Counters piled high with

Parmesans, Taleggios, Romanos. Freshly made pastas — bite-sized raviolis stuffed with ricotta or seafood. Or *medaglione*, silver-dollar-sized pockets of pasta plumped with meat or cheese. Or *gnocchi di patate* — tiny potato dumplings to be smothered in sauce. Coarse fragrant breads. Trays of sweet or spicy sausages to accompany golden polenta.

Nicola, Milano's butcher of thirty years, offers milk-fed spring lamb, guinea hens, rabbits, goat meat. A vast selection of groceries . . . an astonishment of tomato sauces and olive oils. Consider the pizza breads — *olio*, with oil and spices — *napolitana*, with tomatoes — imagine them stuffed with anchovies or sausage. Angelo, the manager, and Bruno, the cheese-man, preside over the counters and absolutely dote over their customers. Long live Milano!

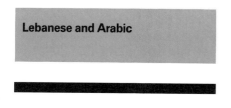

Lebanese and Arabic

Les Aliments Beyrouth
7490 Berri Street
Montreal H2R 2G5
270-7600

Armenia, today, is an uncomfortable member of the Soviet Union. Her history is scarred by invasion, turmoil and genocide that is never far from the lips of Montreal's Armenian community. Ever-changing boundaries and invading armies have infused Armenian cuisine with Greek, Turkish and even Persian influences.

The family history of the Esrabians is similar to one told by many Armenians now in Montreal. Having migrated from Armenia to Turkey, the family escaped the Turkish genocide of Armenians in 1914. They fled to Lebanon, only to arrive on time for the bloody civil war. In 1977, they came to Montreal and established two bustling businesses — a bakery and a grocery store — that seem to employ the entire, very congenial, Esrabian family. The grocery, Les Aliments Beyrouth, sits kitty-corner to the family bakery, Lahmadjoun Beyrouth.

The friendly Esrabian family are delighted to teach the uninformed about Armenian and Lebanese food products. Should you arrive at the same time as the fresh almonds, buy as many as your purse will afford. These pale green, unripened nuts, to be sprinkled with coarse salt, taste slightly peachy, slightly mysterious and altogether sensuous.

Try some unsalted cheese, sold in large slabs. This soft cheese is used for making Armenian string cheese by a sort of taffy-pull process. There's *labneh*, a yogurt-based cheese shaped into balls and immersed in a fragrant brine. Armenian and Lebanese children have *mahalabia*, a custard-like dish, for breakfast . . . look for the colorful packages. Another breakfast specialty available here is Armenian dry biscuits — to be dipped in warmed milk.

Phoenicia Adonis Impex
9590 de L'Acadie Boulevard
St. Laurent H4N 1L8
382-8606

The premier store among the many in the Lebanese-Arab communities is Adonis, located in the tiny Plaza L'Acadie just south of Sauvé. A visit to Adonis is a step through a curtain to another country . . . suddenly the sights and smells are different and intriguing. Instead of packaged white bread . . . mounds of pita, piles of *menahis*, a flat, thin pita doused with olive oil, thyme and sesame seeds . . . baskets of croissants layered with

Strings of freshly made merguez sausage

thyme. No junk food here, just stacks of halawa, rock sugar candy, plump dried fruits, pistachios, sugared chickpeas and sunflower seeds.

The cheese counter at Adonis is one of the best in the city, and because it contains so many astonishing Middle Eastern delicacies it's even more fascinating. Aside from mountains of every conceivable type of feta, two cheeses deserve mention. One is the twisted Armenian cheese speckled with spice . . . pull it apart to reveal delicious strings of salty cheese. Another is the *chankleeh*, a little mound of cheese filled with spice and rolled in oregano. A lovely surprise, found near the cheese counter, are fresh Lebanese crêpes made with flour, water and salt. These fat, little crêpes

are ready to be stuffed with ricotta and walnuts, rolled and doused with honey or fig syrup.

Pastries are made on the premises and feature a marvelous assortment of baklava — all shapes and sizes and fillings. Look for the spinach turnovers. Buy dozens to freeze. The meat department features traditional sausages, like merguez, and kibbe, a Middle Eastern meatball. Large tubs hold Lebanese olives and marinated turnips, a popular appetizer.

Browsing the grocery shelves is a visit to a souk . . . oils from Lebanon, tamarind syrup, fig jam, orange-blossom water, Persian tobacco for water pipes, a maze of exotic, brightly colored couscous packages. Gleaming

brass coffee tables, couscoussières, Oriental coffee makers, backgammon sets and mysterious multi-armed water pipes attract the buyer's eye.

Elie Cheaib and his two partners greet the customer and patiently explain how to use and serve their products. Adonis is a full-scale supermarket, yet like no other in Quebec.

Super Marché Suidan
1545 Henri Bourassa West
Montreal H3M 1X6
331-9915

Minutes from Adonis, Suidan is a slightly smaller Middle Eastern supermarket. Although Suidan has many of the same products as Adonis, the meat department offers a few unique items. Suidan has a large counter of marinated meats for barbecuing and shish kebab. Consider chicken breasts marinating in yogurt and spices. Check out the freezer for frozen *mouloukhia*, an Eygptian spinach, and for huge Iranian tobacco leaves for your water pipe.

Oriental

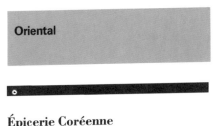

Épicerie Coréenne
6151 Sherbrooke Street West
N.D.G. H4B 1L9
487-1672

West-enders too lazy to make the trip to Chinatown will find everything they need for Oriental cuisine at this modern, new "superette." The growing Oriental community in N.D.G. and Montreal West is creating a small explosion of new stores in the West End.

Épicerie Coréenne has marvelously exotic produce like four-foot-long strips of seaweed, enormous, ear-like shiitake mushrooms and long, purple Japanese eggplants. This shop stocks a number of freezer items of interest to last-minute hosts — tricolor *kamaboko*, or fishcakes, in white, pink and pale green . . . plump vegetable dumplings and sweet red bean buns ready to fry. Nagasaki Castella, a fancy packaged cake, or, per- haps, dried persimmons for dessert.

_____

Sun Sing Lung
72A de La Gauchetière Street West
Montreal H2X 1P5
861-0815

Succulent Chinese barbecue available here — strips of barbecued pork bathed in spices and honey-glazed — roasted meats rubbed with sesame oil and seared to form a crust. Trays hold little bamboo-wrapped packages of rice, golden, deep-fried breadsticks and crispy egg rolls.

_____

Super Marché Luen Hing
1050 St. Laurent Boulevard
Montreal H2Z 1J5
875-1806

The windows of Luen Hing are an irresistible attraction — a mouth- watering seduction scene of golden glazed chickens, ducks with parchment-crisp mahogany skins, whole roast pigs encased in a crackling honey-colored skin, bright-orange barbecued baby octopus. Sunday, the traditional shopping day in Chinatown, finds Luen Hing packed with customers — their carriages laden with oranges, bags of straw mushrooms, bok choy and small children.

Luen Hing is a complete Oriental supermarket with grocery, meat, fish, fruit and vegetable departments. Fruits and vegetables are in superb condition, reflecting their importance in Chinese cuisine.

Occidental visitors are intrigued with the exotica — charred-looking cloud ear mushrooms, preserved eggs cakey with lime and ashes, silver-gray dried abalone and fish's maw, the dried and deep-fried stomach lining of fish used for soup. A flattened preserved duck — boned, pressed and bagged. Brightly colored pink, green and yellow shrimp chips — the Chinese potato chip. Wonderful, delicate plastic boxes filled with licoriced lemon or candied plums or prune candy.

Drama: the cutting of a huge winter melon — one slash with a lethal cleaver reveals the meaty white flesh. Always on Sunday in Chinatown.

Spanish

Libreria Espanola
3811 St. Laurent Boulevard
Montreal H2W 1X9
849-3383

Spanish is spoken here. Serrano hams hang from hooks, gorgeous earthenware crockery adorns the shelves. Try a jar of *mole* paste, the essential Mexican dynamite made of chilies, tomatoes, nuts, squash seeds and a soupçon of chocolate. Red, white and blue sacks of Cruz de Malta, a tea-like leaf favored by Argentineans, are a staple here. Brewed, the beverage is served in gourds which the shop also stocks. Look for frozen tortilla shells and banana leaves for preparing *hallacas* – small packages of meat and vegetables. Quince jelly, to be served with cheese, is found in several varieties. The Galician-born owners attract a small crowd with a selection of Spanish videos, cassettes, books and greeting cards.

West/East Indian

Les Aliments Tropical Foods
6841 Victoria Avenue
Snowdon H3W 2T3
733-2332

If you have a sweet tooth to fill, fill up at Tropical Foods just up the street from Boulangerie Spicee. The courtly Mr. Dhiru Patel, formerly of Bombay, keeps his cooler jammed with colorful, homemade East Indian cakes. Try a few *jalebe*, swirls of sticky, fried orange pastry. Or *garee*, very sweet squares of cake. Don't miss the *samosas* – small patties filled with vegetables – the perfect hors d'oeuvre.

Épicerie Exotique
6495 Victoria Avenue
Snowdon H3W 2S9
738-9775

The windows of Épicerie Exotique are plastered with screaming, iridescent signs announcing "COW FOOT 99c," "PIG SNOUTS 99c," or "GOAT MEAT $1.99 LB." The store is a miniature United Nations of cuisine, with a clientele from Spain, the Caribbean, the Philippines and Africa.

Should you crave palm nut cream soup from Ghana, this is the place to shop. Shiny, green *callaloo*, Jamaican spinach, is set next to bitter melon leaves from the Philippines. Who could resist the 99 cent special on Irish moss? The friendly owner of Exotique sends one off with instructions to boil it down, add condensed milk and take the Island cure.

Sample the hardo bread – a heavy and hard bread that stays fresh for a week. There's a counter full of everything needed to make roti – fresh goat meat, salted beef, oxtail, cow foot and a variety of Island salted fish. Buy yourself a box of Jamaican crackers to go with the salted herring. Wash it all down with some Island ginger beer.

Jean's West Indian
6058 Sherbrooke Street West
N.D.G. H4A 1Y1
489-2146

Ask how to prepare a breadfruit at Jean's – six people with six different accents and six skin colors will be happy to tell you. "This is the way we do it in St. Barts." "No, this is the way in Jamaica." "What you talking about, girl, in Barbados we . . ."

Go to Jean's around 5 p.m. when the little shop becomes an Island community center. Jean, herself, is a great attraction – an astonishing source of recipes, gossip and news. She'll help you tell the dasheen from the baddos, the coco yam from the yampi.

Try Jean's homemade beef patties and ask for roti with curried beef, chicken or goat – which she will produce miraculously from her back store kitchen. Although Jean stocks bottles and bottles of red-hot pepper sauce, she dismisses them as "baby food." She dares you to try her homemade pepper sauce and a thimbleful of her chutney. No baby food these.

Jean with her dasheen, baddos and yampis

N.D.G. Licensed Grocery
5345 Sherbrooke Street West
N.D.G. H4A 1V2
481-3034

A few doors west of Sol's . . . tucked right under the arm of N.D.G. Meat Market. Bright green mangoes and ruby red Scotch bonnet peppers are displayed against a backdrop of somber brown yams and cassava. This tiny shop has some of the best-looking Island produce in town.

Sol's Fruits et Épicerie
5331 Sherbrooke Street West
N.D.G. H4A 1V2
486-6566

Sol Yurbin is probably the only Orthodox, Yiddish-speaking Caribbean grocer in Montreal. He's been on Sherbrooke near Décarie for 48 years and watched as his clientele became predominately "Island people." Sol makes it clear that "these are not my customers, these are my friends." He worries that big stores "don't give a good damn about people." Sol does, and he cares enough to know the minutiae of Caribbean dietary laws. His Bajan friends will demand flying fish; his Jamaican friends won't touch it.

Sol stocks a variety of West Indian produce – breadfruit, peppery, little Scotch bonnet peppers, sugarcane, yams and other tubers. Jamaican

cheese, a Gouda made from an ancient Dutch recipe, is an Island favorite stocked here. There are dense, golden sweet buns and delicious Island cakes perfumed with coconut. Mag's Improved Creole Seasoning is one of many intriguing, and fiery, sauces from the Islands. Salted beef and pork, pig tails and snouts, goat meat and salted fish fill the back store counters.

I asked Sol how he reconciled his own dietary laws with the handling of pork products. "Well, I have to make a living," he reflected. "A dead man can't praise the Lord."

Sol, the only Yiddish-speaking Caribbean grocer in Montreal

Takeout

The variety of prepared foods available for takeout in Montreal has moved well beyond Chinese food and smoked meat. Make a meal of *lahmadjoun*, or golden, flaky beef patties, perhaps some falafel, or Portuguese barbecue. Should you be in a high tech mood, the new wave is vacuum-packed cuisine . . . *flan de volaille périgourdin* or, perhaps, *terrine de saumon et homard.*

There are shops which will prepare an entire calendar of menus, those who will fill your freezer, and many which will give you a day off from cooking. These people enjoy feeding you. Eat. Enjoy.

Baking lahmadjoun *in the aromatic wood-fired oven*

Canadian

Allô J'ai Faim
4430 St. Laurent Boulevard
Montreal H2W 1Z5
287-1935

This stark takeout shop with the up-front name is the creation of veteran caterer Gisèle Gauthier. She's added the words "boutique de prêt à manger" to the vocabulary. Vacuum-packed pouches, which lock in flavor, are filled with entrées like *panache de la mer* or beef *bourguignon*. Simply immerse for five minutes in boiling water. There are also vegetables, desserts and appetizers to be prepared in the same manner. Most items come packaged in portions for one or two people.

This shop could become a secret resource for singles who love to entertain but, alas, can only boil water. If you can't boil water, Gisèle will cater.

La Binerie Mont Royal
367 Mont Royal East
Montreal H2T 1R1
285-9078

Generations of school kids growing up near Mont Royal and St. Denis have filled their lunch pails at La Binerie. The Lussier and Groulx families have baked beans here for the last fifty years.

Beans, and pork and beans. Beans and tourtières — real tourtière, half pork and half beef. Ragout with meatballs slathered with gravy. Good pâté chinois. Dishes you haven't seen for a long time — like blanc-mange, an old-fashioned custard. Try a *sandwich au lard salé*. Be sure to drench your beans in maple syrup. And ask for some homemade pickles to go.

Check out the ancient photo over the cash of La Binerie decades ago. Nothing has changed. Clean arborite tables and counters. All beans and all business. Eat in or take out.

Coin du Traiteur
900 Rachel Street East
Montreal H2J 2S1
521-0271

Out of the way, but those in the know have the phone number of this trendy, neighborhood shop. Jean-Marie Gaultier, trained in the classic cuisine of his native Val de Loire, and his Quebec-born wife, Diane, cook takeout meals for smart uptown addresses. Meals are prepared in one-portion servings . . . so fill up the freezer with hearty soups, *filet de turbot Crécy*, *navarin d'agneau*, or seafood *coquilles*. The boutique also offers French-cut meat, a basic choice of cheese, vegetables and groceries. A large part of the business is catering. Speak to Diane.

Gourmaison
5519 Côte St. Luc Road
Côte St. Luc H3X 2C6
481-4336

Gourmaison offers total convenience . . . serious meals for singles, retired folk and people stocking up the city or country freezer. Nathan and Liz prepare both freezer and fresh meals

SPÉCIALITÉ → FÈVES au LARD

SOUPE, BREUVAGE, POUDING	CRETONS 4.55	SANDW. AU JAMBON 2.00	DEJEUNERS
JUS DE TOMATE	JAMBON FROID 4.55	SANDW. au LARD SAL. 3.25	CRÊPES u CAFÉ 2.60
POT. au LÉGUMES	ROTI PORC FROID 4.5	SANDW. aux CRETONS	TOAST · PAIN · CROUTÉ
MACARONI A VIANDE 3.25	STEAK HACHE 4.55	SANDW. PORC FRAIS...	JUS D'ORANGES 75¢
COEUR DE VEAU 3.60	LARD SALÉ FROID 4.5	DESSERTS .80	TOAST + FÈVES + CAFÉ
FOIE DE PORC 4.10	TOURTIÈRE RAGOUT · FÈVES 5.70	TARTE AUX POMMES	2 OEUFS FRITS
BOEUF AUX LÉGUMES 4.30	RIB STEAK 6.60	TARTE AUX RAISINS	PATATES FRICASSÉES
SPAGHETTI 4.35		TARTE AU COCONUT	OMELETTES
BOEUF AUX FÈVES 4.30	SAUCISSES au PORC 4.30	TARTE AUX FRAISES	
TOURTIERE 4.30	CORNICHONS MAISON 50		BLANC MANGE
PATÉ CHINOIS 4.30	BETTERAVES .50		PUDDING · CHOMEUR
RAGOUT DE BOULETTES 4.30	GRAISSE DE ROTI .7		PUDDING AU PAIN
ROTI de BOEUF 4.75	FÈVES AU LARD 75 EXT		

FÈVES au LARD
Pain / Breuvage

for those who will not or cannot cook. It's not unusual for singles to stock up on oven-ready, microwave-packaged meals, for a month of carefree dining.

There's a weekly takeout menu. If it's Monday, it must be Lemon Chicken; Tuesday, Chicken Satay. Soups, salads, desserts are also conveniently packaged. Custom-designed catering.

Pellatt's Food Market
3630 St. Denis Street
Montreal H2X 3L7
842-4169

A family business since 1910, Pellatt's is changing with St. Denis. Fred and Joy Pellatt are slowly and carefully adapting their small shop to the busy professional of Montreal's Quartier Latin. Aside from groceries, store-baked bread and vegetables, Pellatt's offers a variety of gourmet-to-go comfort foods – Buffalo chicken wings, stuffed artichokes, pâté chinois and homemade soups. A sure bet for good-looking fruit and specialty baskets.

Roger Colas, Traiteur
98 Laurier Avenue West
Outremont H2T 2N4
271-1777

Roger Colas is a young man in a hurry. Since graduating from hotel management school five years ago, he has established himself as one of the city's foremost caterers, having served the Pope, the president of France, the Queen Mum and countless Montreal tycoons. His distinctive black and white vans are parked in front of some of the city's best addresses.

The corner shop on Laurier, east of Park Avenue, serves as an office for the catering business and a small shop for walk-in customers. Each day the counters are filled with a variety of single-portion meals, presented in microwave and oven-proof dishes. It's not unusual for clients to take home dozens of dishes for their freezers. One night it's *terrine de ris de veau* — another, *flan de crabe homardine*. It's a good way to sample a variety of dishes that can be catered. Delicate, pretty canapés for at least six people can be ordered with a few hours' notice. The shop also prepares a number of attractively jarred, homemade chutneys, sauces and preserves.

Roger will cater intimate dinners or gastronomic suppers for a crowd and arrange all the details — from dishes to bartenders.

East European

Bucarest Charcuterie & Pâtisserie
6122 Côte St. Luc Road
Côte St. Luc H3X 2G9
481-4732

Marcel Merimas mans the front end of this friendly shop and his wife runs the kitchen. Roumanian-speaking customers drop in during the week for old country specialties, gossip and Roumanian-language newspapers from New York. On the floor — tubs of prune butter, *lekva*, to be served on bread and sprinkled with walnuts. Try

Roumanian sorbet – a sweet but not frozen confection – spooned into a glass of water and sipped on a langorous summer afternoon.

Traditional sausages like *carnatzl*. Goose *schmaltz*, or fat, for cooking. A very special old country treat – goose pastrami. Dried carp roe – serve sliced as an appetizer. Roumanian strudel – flaky phyllo stuffed with walnuts, orange peel and Turkish delight.

Homemade *chorba* – soup made sour, *à la Roumanie*, with fermented wheat bran. Ecra, eggplant salad, mashed beans with garlic, tripe soup, baby green walnut preserves. Roumanian soul food.

Polka Deli
3561 Bélair Street
Montreal H2A 2B1
727-2311

A small corner of Warsaw transferred to Montreal. A homey, busy deli with all manner of Polish sausage and dried and cured meats. Mittel European groceries. Tables for sandwiches and talk. A bulletin board for information of interest to the Polish community, Polish-language newspapers and videos. Located under a major meeting hall for the community.

Kosher

Chez Foxy
5987 Victoria Avenue
Snowdon H3W 2R9
739-8777

This plain and simple restaurant-takeout place looks as if it could be on any Tel Aviv street corner. Plastered with Hebrew posters announcing concerts and lectures, the shop bustles with activity. Specialties here are strictly kosher. Falafel, the "hamburger" of the Middle East, humous, a puree of chickpeas and sesame oil, and pizza, which requires no explanation.

Knick Nosh
5204 Décarie Boulevard
Snowdon H3X 2H9
481-0331

To "nosh" is a Yiddish term meaning to nibble on food, not quite seriously in the manner of a meal, but not exactly mindlessly. "Noshing" does, however, require interesting material. At Knick Nosh, the reincarnation of the Prestige Kosher Catering company, the nosher will discover some interesting noshes. Several types of prepared chicken dishes – lemon, Kiev, tempura, and lychee chicken. Veal and beef dishes are well represented. Potatoes, rice and vegetable side dishes are good looking. The shop offers complete take-home menus from soup to dessert. Bread, bagels, candy, cakes and cookies — all kosher, of course — are there for the nosh.

Kosher-style

The Brown Derby
4827 Van Horne Avenue
Snowdon H3W 1J2
739-2331

The Brown Derby is a state of mind — part Damon Runyon, part Grossinger's. A place where time is passed, deals are made, gossip is whispered, secrets are traded. In between, chicken soup is sipped, tons of coleslaw are devoured, mountains of rye bread are plowed under. The Brown Derby is the culinary mecca for those who crave kosher-style, old-fashioned Jewish cooking. The smoked meat is legendary.

A colorful and lively crowd. Take a number at the takeout counter and watch what other people order. ''A jar of chicken soup. Two. No, make it three matzo balls. A pound of coleslaw. You know, I think I'll take some chopped liver. A pound. Throw in some pickles. Gimme half a pound smoked meat. With fat. A nice piece of gefilte fish.'' A small order.

The soups, mostly frozen, are memorable here — especially the robust bean and barley. A large selection of smoked and pickled fish, East European style — herring, salmon, whitefish, baked and boiled carp. Try some *ecra* — a Roumanian specialty of carp or pike

Montreal Kosher Quality Bakery
7005 Victoria Avenue
Snowdon H4Q 2N9
739-3651

A strictly kosher bakery and food store with takeout meals that look and taste homey and good. If you've never tasted gefilte fish or a sweet tzimmes, a carrot pudding, this is the place. Entire meals, in one-portion containers, are available here — kugels, soups, cholent, ribs, chicken. Good Jewish breads and cake. Outstanding old-fashioned, fresh farmer cheese made by Mehedrin's and delivered several times a week. If you don't have a Jewish grandmother, adopt Kosher Quality.

roe. Mighty mounds of gefilte fish —
finely chopped, raw fish mixed with
eggs, cooked and served with pungent
horseradish.

There is an enormous takeout menu
at the Brown Derby — from soup to
desserts. To note: the rice pudding —
golden, raisin-y and creamy. Don't
overlook the frozen food counter —
soups, prepared main courses and,
of course, the cheese bagels. Cheese
bagels — a sort of crêpe formed to
resemble a bagel and stuffed with
farmer cheese — to be fried in butter
and smothered with sour cream.

The Brown Derby is located in the Van
Horne Shopping Center . . . a center
not quite like others — a genuine
neighborhood marketplace. Small
groups of men congregate in knots to
decide the fate of the world and to
argue heatedly about business deals
long done. Have a haircut at Angelo's
Barber Shop — the brain center of
Snowdon — the information nodule of
the Van Horne District. Local color.

Snowdon Delicatessen
5265 Décarie Boulevard
Snowdon H3W 3C2
488-9129

A lively, friendly place. The smoked
meat is probably the best in the city,
vying only with Schwartz's. Stock-in-
trade here is kosher-style food —
chopped liver, pickled salmon, chicken
soup, blintzes, all-veal hot dogs.
Snowdon makes its own whipped

cream cheese and that alone makes
standing in line on Sunday mornings a
pleasure. Snowdon aficionados debate
whether the apple-cherry strudel or the
apple squares are ''the best'' and
usually take home both. The schmaltz
herring and matjes herring are
specialties of the house.

Lebanese

Lahmadjoun Beyrouth
420 Faillon Street
Montreal H2R 1L4
270-1076

Lahmadjoun is an Armenian fast food,
a crispy round of dough, thinner than
pizza, spread with ground beef and
onions and baked in an aromatic wood
fire. The fragrant smell of the wood fire
adds to the intense flavor of another
specialty, *zataar* — a doughy base
slathered with oil and thyme and
studded with fennel seeds. Cut into
slivers, it makes a spicy and addictive
hors d'oeuvre.

Taste the *fatayar* — doughy triangles
filled with spinach, meat or cheese —
piled high on the counters. The
Esrabian family say that they are the
only ones in Montreal to make a
Lebanese cheesecake called *kenafé* —
available only on weekends. At Easter,
and on special occasions, they bake
maamoul — a torpedo-shaped pastry
made from dates and pistachios.

The wood-burning brick oven is the centerpiece of the shop. Logs stacked in the front window add a rustic decoration to a simple shop. I predict that *lahmadjoun* shops will become the latest Montreal food obsession. The crunch of the parchment-like crust, the zing of the steaming, spicy meat filling – a taste very easily acquired.

The women of the Esrabian family prepare dough for lahmadjoun.

Restaurant Zahle
1465 Dudemaine Street
St. Laurent H3M 1P9
336-3013

Plan to stop here for lunch and sample some of the Armenian and Lebanese specialties available to take out. Spinach *fatayar*, or Armenian "pizza," a crisp piece of dough spread with meat, tomatoes and onions. Call ahead to Terry . . . she'll prepare an order of *yabrabk* – grape leaves stuffed with rice, meat and vegetables. Terry also keeps dozens of tiny meat pies, *sambosic*, ready for her party-loving Lebanese customers. Make room in the freezer before you visit Zahle.

South American

BBQ Charcuterie "Coco Rico"
also known as Rico Castanheira
3907 St. Laurent Boulevard
Montreal H2W 1X9
849-5554

No one would be capable of walking past the steaming window of this barbecue specialist and ignoring the stacks of Portuguese breads and the smoky aroma of meat on the grill. Never again Chalet This or That. Coco Rico should be the first stop for assembling an informal meal. Barbecued chickens with golden, crackling skins. Sizzling slabs of fragrant pork ribs. Add a Portuguese bread and a green salad. Buy a six-pack and invite the boys.

West Indian

Boulangerie Spicee
6889A Victoria Avenue
Snowdon H3W 2T3
739-9714

Follow your nose down the steps to the best little beef patties in town. Hordes of schoolchildren with musical Island accents run to Boulangerie Spicee at the sound of the noontime bell. Spicee is the name of the baker. He makes fat golden patties and stuffs them with curry-scented ground beef. Two will fill up a schoolchild just perfectly. Take home a few patties and an order of roti, a flat Indian bread stuffed with curried chicken or beef. The cooler is amply stocked with ginger beer and malta, a malt beverage popular throughout the Caribbean. Plan to arrive around noon and watch Spicee's helpers make roti.

A note: One would think that it would be easy to find French-Canadian specialties to take out in Montreal . . . not so. It seems that the best tourtières, boulettes and fèves are made at home. Two spots of note outside of Montreal are Les Beignets Dora in Eastman, Quebec, known for tourtières, doughnuts and pies. And Brasserie Raftman, the place to go for fèves au lard in Hull, Quebec.

Health Food

Health food stores have vastly improved their image in the past few years. Shelves have been dusted, packaging has become colorful and seductive, and fresh organic fruits and vegetables are attractive and affordable. Many of these stores have expanded their repertoire to include prepared foods and bulk grains and legumes. True, some of the hocus-pocus still exists — the herbal brews to purify blood, the dreadful drinks to replace milk — but that just adds to the fun of shopping at the health food store.

Tisanes, herbs and health remedies stock a health store window.

**Le Commensal Cuisine
Végétarienne**
2115 St. Denis Street
Montreal H2X 3K8
845-2627

680 St. Catherine Street West
Montreal H3B 1C2
871-1480

Le Commensal restaurants, bakery
and takeout are a Way of Life. A food
religion . . . organic vegetables being
the true path to either a higher spiritual
life or better digestion. A variety of
good veg meals to take out. Good-
looking, down-home cakes, muffins,
breads and cookies. The kind of stuff
that would do a Vermont bake sale
proud.

Mission Santé Thuy
1138 Bernard Avenue West
Outremont H2V 1V3
272-9386

This is an efficient, bustling, yet warm
natural food store – probably the best
and most appealing in the city. A large
portion of the store is given to
medicinal herbs, natural vitamins and
cosmetics. White-uniformed Mme
Bach-Tuyet Royer dispenses products
and information.

There is an appetizing selection of
organic vegetables and bulk health
food such as organic flour and
legumes. And of course, the esoterica

of health food – the blue tortilla chips,
the cactus salad dressings. Oriental
and vegetarian takeout meals are
popular here – beautiful sushi, all-
vegetable lasagna. A vast choice of
organic dairy products and bread.

Mont Blanc Herbalist
3489 St. Laurent Boulevard
Montreal H2X 2T6
288-8728

Look for the turquoise and gold façade
and the 4711 Cologne sign hanging
over the entrance. This tiny herbalist
has the most elegant storefront on a

Liniments for aches and pains

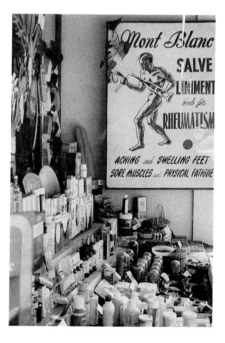

decidedly undistinguished part of the Main. A charming, Zurich-born lady has attended to the shop's predominately Swiss-German clientele for forty years. Soft Swiss-German accents make you feel that you've wandered down a Zurich side street.

Shelves filled with blackthorn elixir, blueberry juice and dandelion coffee substitute. Mont Blanc has its own tisane blends labeled, quite forthrightly, in the Swiss manner, "#2," or "#3." Choose #3 "to purify the blood," #18 to "aid in elimination." A jar of "nerve elixir" will relieve the effects of a bad week.

Tau Natural Foods Grocery
4238 St. Denis Street
Montreal H2J 2K8
843-4420

Because of their "mission," health food stores are generally not appetizing. One has to be a total convert to find a dusty can of Dandelion Hot Drink Blend an unbearable temptation. "Tau," however, dispels the musty, stuffy image. It's a lively place – probably one of the busiest stores on a busy part of St. Denis.

Along with the obligatory psyllium husks, reputed to be a "colon cleanser" by the cognoscenti, one will find top-notch, organically grown fruits and vegetables and a wide range of organic dairy products.

The groceries are interesting. There is a tempting choice of slickly packaged health foods from the United States and Japan. Also, prepared appetizers like sushi, humous, baba ghannouj and tabbouleh. Bulk honeys, barley malt, peanut butter, legumes, flours and rice of every variety. Freshly baked organic breads of all descriptions. Take home a "Bible bread" and get religion.

Pasta

Pasta is probably the quintessential food of the eighties. When historians examine our eating patterns, they will note that pasta is to the eighties what quiche was to the seventies. Pasta probably doesn't deserve the comparison; after all it has a long and reputable history. Fresh pasta can be found in all parts of the city, in all the new upscale food markets, and even in supermarket counters. We've gone beyond spaghetti, and even fettuccine. We've discovered gnocchi and *medaglione* and life will never be the same.

Benito Paralovo, master pasta-maker, of La Casa dei Ravioli

La Casa dei Ravioli
2479 Charland Avenue
Montreal North H1Z 1C3
381-2481

Italian mamas who don't make their own pasta beat a path to Casa dei Ravioli. A hidden gem of Montreal's North End. The spotless, factory-like shop, owned by partners Benito Paralovo and Giuseppe Sacchetto, makes serious pasta. The two Venice-born partners trained in Turin and came to Canada thirteen years ago to start their business.

Watch as pounds and pounds of fettuccine are cranked from huge machines. Piles of meat- or cheese-stuffed tortellini fill wooden bins. *Gnocchi di patate* — tiny, delicate potato dumplings — are airy and light. Wonderfully named *capelli d'angelo*, or "angel's hair," is fragile and weightless. Ask for the *medaglione*, medallion-sized rounds of pasta stuffed with meat and cheese, and the ravioli stuffed with cheese. Plan to fill your freezer here — pasta freezes well.

Mr. Sacchetto smacks his lips, in that particularly Italian gesture, as he recommends the bread at Boulangerie Sylvia, 9099 Iberville, H1Z 2R2, 389-8723.

Combine a visit to La Casa dei Ravioli with a stop at four other Charland Avenue stores to complete your shopping excursion. Marché Charland (at 2339) is a congenial Italian dépanneur and has just the right Parmigiano to grate over your pasta. Poissonnerie Scilla (at 2301A) has good-looking fish. Agricon (at 2275) will provide you with huge barrels and wine-making ingredients. And Boulangerie & Pâtisserie Salerno (at 2411) has lusty, crusty Italian breads, huge flat slabs of pizza and rococo pastry. Should you be traveling in Montreal North at 3 a.m., Salerno is open 24 hours a day.

Épicerie Fine Al Dente
5767 Monkland Avenue
N.D.G. H4A 1E8
486-4343

Tiny Al Dente produces fresh pasta for the Monkland shopping district. Several varieties of pasta and sauces are prepared each day. Also to note: pizzarelli, tiny triangles of dough filled with cheese. And plump ratatouille or spinach-filled calzone.

Italissimo
615 Bloomfield Avenue
Outremont H2V 3S2
270-8600

A mini-shop, just big enough for a counter and a freezer which holds prepared takeout meals. Dependable fresh pasta and tomato-y sauces. A variety of home-cooked meals either fresh or frozen. Of note here — the La Contadina line of jarred Italian specialties like pesto, porcini mushroom paste and *sugoloso*, an Italian condiment. Feel free to bring your own pan to be filled with lasagna, cannelloni or other party pasta dishes. Just off the Bernard scene.

Pastadoro
5456 Jean Talon East
Montreal H1S 1L6
729-2021

A tiny shop located in the bustling Italian neighborhood of Jean Talon East. The shop sells pasta and pasta sauces and not a thing else. They mean business. Fettuccine, cappelletti, cavatelli, lasagna leaves, gnocchi – all manner of fresh pasta prepared daily for busy cooks.

Restaurant Magnani
9245 Lajeunesse Street
Montreal H2M 1S3
387-5959

A flash of red neon on a rather colorless part of Lajeunesse screams out "Magnani Restaurant." The waiter proudly notes that Magnani, at age thirty-four, is the "oldest Italian restaurant in Montreal" – careful to make a distinction between Magnani and the nouveau "brochetteries" that serve lasagna and audaciously call themselves "Italian."

A well-worn place . . . a perfectly preserved forties period piece. Divided into two dining areas – one dark

paneled and the other lit by fluorescent, revealing hospital-green walls and checkered tablecloths. The "decor package" works. Perfect movie set for a romance in a gritty Northern Italian automobile town. Let's hope no one ever updates Magnani.

The front end of the green dining room is a small store devoted to fresh pasta and homemade sauces. Magnani is well known to old-time pasta aficionados . . . in the past, one of the few Montreal places to buy fresh pasta. These days fresh pasta can be found in most every corner of the city. But there is something about Magnani's. If you're in the area drop in. Cheaper than a trip to Turin.

The finished product

Chocolate

There are some Montrealers who remember the great Léonie chocolate shop that once graced Sherbrooke at St. Denis. Today there are still a few chocolatiers in Montreal. And their ranks are often joined by well-trained newcomers to Canada who make chocolate according to ancient recipes brought from the old country. Chocolate lovers persist in rehashing the Great Chocolate Debate — whether dark chocolate or milk chocolate brings one closest to chocolate paradise. Chocolate is making a comeback in Montreal.

Madeleine and her box of temptations

Chocolats Andrée
5328 Park Avenue
Montreal H2V 4G7
279-5923

4144 St. Catherine Street West
Westmount H3Z 1P4
937-1814

1520 Fleury Street East
Montreal H2C 1S4
387-8969

Madeleine Farond trained at the
Montreal "Mother House" of
chocolate, Léonie. Once an institution
on Sherbrooke at St. Denis and later on
Mountain Street, Léonie no longer
exists. Chocolats Andrée is its spiritual
successor. Madeleine opened her first
shop forty-eight years ago, when Park
Avenue was quite a fashionable
boulevard. She recalls all the "great"
Montreal families who have passed
through over the years.

Andrée's hand-dipped chocolates
contain no preservatives. The majority
of pieces are made with dark, dark
chocolate. Madeleine says that those
who "understand" chocolate will eat
only dark chocolate. The shop's most
popular piece is a dark chocolate with
a caramel filling. And that's caramel
made with thirty-five percent cream,
Madeleine is quick to point out. The
shop makes fanciful chocolate baskets
to fill with truffles for a dinner centerpiece. The boxes are imported from
Europe, rotated according to season
and make an elegant presentation.

And who is Andrée? Andrée is
Madeleine. To be exact Marie
Madeleine Cecile Andrée Farond. Of all
her names Madeleine likes Andrée the
best.

Le Chocolat Belge Heyez
Place Bonaventure Passage CN
1000 de La Gauchetière West
Montreal H2L 2W5
392-1480

The underground shopping passage at
Place Bonaventure is made more
palatable after one discovers Le
Chocolat Belge Heyez. The two Heyez,
père et fils, make their chocolate
extravaganzas at their St. Bruno shop.
Charles Heyez, père, had been a

master chocolate-maker in Belgium for forty years before coming to Canada two years ago.

Heyez uses only Callebaut chocolate from Belgium for coatings. Centers are made from good Québécois materials. Chocolates are sent right to Montreal after daily production, ensuring their freshness. Many of the centers are made with fresh cream, in the Belgian style, and flavored with Cointreau or kirsch or lemon . . . There's a gin fizz — lemon mousse flavored with a shot of gin and enrobed in dark chocolate.

A marvelous "grenoblois" requires description — a chocolate half filled with walnut paste and topped with a walnut half. Beautiful. Chocolates come in some seventy different flavors . . . although some on a seasonal basis.

Heyez can carve any shape from chocolate, although they do have 200 molds. Occasionally they are asked to do the unusual piece — for Easter, a windmill with revolving chocolate blades. Pâtes de fruits, those jellied fruits so favored by Europeans, are also made by Heyez.

Tourists exploring Montreal's underground city discovered this shop long before les Montréalais. What a pity!

Le Fameux Chocolat Belge LOS
605 de Maisonneuve Boulevard West
Montreal H3A 1L8
849-2620

Belgian chocolate-makers take their business very seriously, intuitively understanding the correct balance between chocolate, butter, creams and flavorings. Belgium-born Nicole Gaevart decided to plunge into the chocolate market two years ago. Nicole becomes spirited when she discusses the Montreal chocolate scene — the inferior products, the abuse of the Belgian appellation, the high-priced French-snob-appeal chocolates, the less-than-fresh Belgian product sold by large department stores.

Nicole imports and sells from her shop the very fine product of the House of Léonidas, Brussels. One taste of "Manon" and you are converted. Baptism by chocolate. White chocolate hiding a dollop of mocha cream resting on a praline crust. Real white chocolate — no vegetable oil, no, heaven forbid, paraffin. Just extra cocoa butter. One forgives Nicole a thousand times over for her unabashed preference for Belgian products — the superior dark chocolate, the rich cream that makes even richer butter, the true flavors that translate into divine morsels.

No freshness problem here. Nicole's Brussels-based sister rushes freshly made chocolates to a waiting Sabena flight, every Thursday at 6 a.m. Nicole receives them at noon at Mirabel. By 4 p.m. they are carefully arranged in the counter in her downtown Montreal shop. At 5 p.m., watch the well-dressed gentlemen carefully select ballotins of chocolate. The silver beribboned white boxes, filled with their chocolate jewels, are then sealed with hot red wax. Are that many Montreal wives surprised by elegant packages of chocolate each evening?

Packaging is very important. The boxes are changed with the seasons. Also note the Limoges porcelain hearts — large enough for six truffles. The tiny "house" boxes — perfect for after-dinner surprises.

Mixing a vat of dark chocolate at Andrée's

A simple shop . . . nothing to distract the chocolate lover from the ultimate goal. Behind the Bay. Impossible to park. I would get here in a storm.

Finesse Chocolate
5945 Victoria Avenue
Snowdon H3W 2R9
735-1925

Kosher chocolate heaven. The Stutmans have been making and shaping chocolates for the nicest tables for the last six years. Dipping ginger, dipping strawberries. Hand dipping is an art. The center must be coated quickly and evenly — not too thin, not too thick. Finesse specializes in unique chocolate creations made, of course, by hand, without benefit of molds, baskets, bottles, miniature houses. Unique centerpieces for Sweet Sixteens and weddings. Marvelous chocolate dessert cups to fill with strawberries and cream. Finesse does good-looking fruit and chocolate baskets.

Stilwell's Home Made Candy
5123 Wellington Street
Verdun H4G 1Y2
766-4481

Stilwell's is a child of the Depression. The little store in Verdun hasn't changed a bit since it opened to sell homemade candy in 1934. The white candy boxes are the same, the counters are original, the coke-fired stove is still in use and, best of all, the humbugs are the same. Yes, the humbugs — the same buttery, minty candies developed from an old family recipe — the signature candy of the Stilwell business. But it's the Stilwell fudge bar that started the business — a fudge bar made by one Stilwell child and sold by another, door to door, throughout the Great Depression.

Today, the range extends beyond fudge bars and humbugs, although humbugs remain the all-time favorite. Drop in for hand-dipped chocolates . . . choose among sixty different chocolate centers. Crunchy old-fashioned peanut brittle, toffee, cherry blossoms, clove candy.

Make the pilgrimage to Wellington Street . . . take a child and a grandmother. Kay (née Stilwell), her daughter, Connie, and her son, John, are delightful. The family says it won't change a thing . . . if they did they would have to learn how to make candy all over again. Closed July and August. Stock up before.

La Truffe Belge
5108 Sherbrooke Street West
N.D.G. H4A 1T1
482-0607

This tiny shop goes through 5,000 pounds of chocolate between Christmas and Valentine's Day. Pounds and pounds of French mint, Grand Marnier, white chocolate truffles go to lucky hips. Proprietor Virginia Bostock's Belgian ancestry makes her loyal to pure Belgian milk chocolate. Luscious, velvety chocolate truffle cakes, hazelnut tortes and golden cheesecakes can be ordered with one day's notice. Fill one of the shop's stylish pink boxes with white and chocolate "bark." Get into bed, lock the door and munch away.

Coffee, Tea, Beverages and Spice

Interest in the little brown coffee bean and the fading gray tea leaf can become intense in some circles. There are those who will pay enormous sums for a pound of Jamaican Blue Mountain coffee beans or the latest leaf from the Himalayan highlands. Esoterica aside . . . it is possible to find in Montreal marvelous, fragrant coffees and teas . . . fresh roasted coffee beans and well-stored loose tea leaves. There do exist a few artisans who work in coffee, who roast every day, who grind to specification and who can tell you their own coffee secrets. Buy your herbs and spice from bulk purveyors. Experiment . . . mix your own curry powder as good cooks do in India or grind your own Mexican *mole* paste.

Coffee, Tea

La Brûlerie St. Denis
3967 St. Denis Street
Montreal H2W 2M4
286-9158

If the wind is right, you won't have any trouble finding a fresh cup of coffee on St. Denis Street. The centerpiece of this sparkling new, white-tiled shop is a huge coffee roaster, big enough to pull a trainload of tourists up the Swiss Alps. Stacks of burlap bags filled with green coffee beans wait their turn at the roaster.

There is a vast selection of decaffein-ated coffees, both chemically and water washed. Hard to find Jamaican Blue Mountain is available just below the price of gold. All the trendy flavored roasts are here — amaretto, vanilla, hazelnut — everything but eggplant.

The chalkboard coffee list reads like the index of National Geographic — Ethiopian Harrar, Zimbabwe Code 053, Costa Rica Hard. Try the house blend — a medium, dark roast — fragrant and lingering. A wide selection of specialty teas and infusions here. (Products also available at Ogilvy's basement, 1307 St. Catherine Street West, H3G 1P7.)

Gérard Van Houtte
1042 Laurier Avenue West
Outremont H2V 2K8
274-5601

The granddaddy of the various Van Houtte chains. Coffee beans were once roasted above the shop. This Van Houtte features a wide range of coffee beans and coffee-making paraphernalia and tea leaves. Aside from a large choice of standard cheeses and undistinguished pâtés, the shop has a vast selection of imported specialty items — hard-to-find mustards, candied violets, exotic fruit vinegars and esoteric French pastas. Cousin bread is delivered here daily.

Rio Coffee
217 St. Viateur Street West
Montreal H2T 2L6
273-1478

Rio Coffee is hidden among the many old world treasures of St. Viateur Street — one street east of the Bagel Factory. A minuscule shop — its storefront no bigger than a door and a tiny show window. A handsome, bright yellow sign announces the corporate head-quarters of Rio Coffee — the pride of its owners, Litsa and Louis Papavasiliou. The couple has been roasting beans, grinding coffee, answering the phone and serving customers for thirty-two years. Litsa says her coffee is the best in Montreal.

Critical of the ubiquitous Montreal coffee chain, Litsa confesses that she's "not looking to be a millionaire." She cuts no corners, uses a blend of the best beans available and roasts three or four times a week. Rio is good, fresh, aromatic coffee. The place, with shop, office, warehouse and roaster all in one room, is worth a visit on its own. A couple of pounds of Rio Coffee is an added bonus.

Union Coffee Products
148 Jean Talon West
Montreal H2R 2X1
273-5555

The Kouri family stoked up their coffee roaster in 1927 and hasn't stopped it yet. Eric Kouri now runs the business at the edge of the Jean Talon Market. One thousand pounds of coffee go through the roaster daily, permeating the corner of Jean Talon and Clark with an enticing robust aroma. A steady stream of workers from nearby buildings crowd the espresso bar for their steaming cup of morning coffee.

Union does the bulk of its business in the restaurant trade with its popular Rainbow blend. Retail customers can pick up a pound, too. Or try Eric's favorite blend – one part "espresso bar," one part black Colombian, one part mocha brown, one part brown Colombian. Exquisite gleaming copper Gaggia and Rancilio espresso machines are sold here.

Beverages

Eskimo Bottling Works
6968 Marconi Street
Montreal H2S 3K1
274-7613

Home delivery only. Seltzer unlimited. Wonderful, old-fashioned seltzer bottles etched with the Eskimo logo. Just add natural syrups for a healthy substitute to soft drinks. Deposit required. Usually a minimum order of six.

Gordon's Cave à Vin
5785A Sherbrooke Street West
N.D.G. H4A 1X2
487-2739

7282 St. Hubert Street
Montreal H2R 2N1
271-5786

James Gordon's hobby was wine-making and brewing. Now it's his business. Six years ago, frustrated by a lack of material and information, Gordon went into business. Pick your way through the paraphernalia of the art – kegs, caps, corks, labels – and head for the wine-making kits. Learn to make your own Château Mouton-Rothschild. Homemade wine is all natural, no chemicals, and cheap at $1 or $2 a bottle.

If beer is your thing, pick up the ingredients for German- or English-style malts, lagers, stouts, and black beers. Noirot extracts from France are recommended as flavors for liqueurs to make at home. A soupçon of cinchona and you are in the Dubonnet business. This is a friendly place . . . a meeting place for hobbyists and experts. The staff is tremendously helpful.

canned goods, legumes, rice and spice. Enkin, the king of spice, reigns over a kingdom of 135 varieties. If Enkin doesn't have what you want, no one will.

Turmeric, used extensively in Middle Eastern cuisines, is the biggest mover. There are fresh herbs like *sheba* from Morocco. Reformed smokers buy licorice batons to chew away the urge to smoke. There are all manner of nuts, dried fruits, vegetables, dried fish and marinated salads. Ask for a jar of Enkin's Special Steak Spice — pungent and peppery.

Spice

Anatol Maison des 1000 Épices
6822 St. Laurent Boulevard
Montreal H2S 3C7
276-0107

A no-nonsense kind of place. A sort of warehouse for herbs, spices and some bulk food items such as powdered chicken soup and jello. A short walk from Milano Fruiterie.

World Wide Imported Foods (George Enkin - Le Roi des Épices)
Plaza Côte des Neiges
6700 Côte des Neiges
Montreal H3S 2B2
733-1463

Fight your way into World Wide. And fight to maintain your position. Absorb the sights, smells and colors. Join the crowds jostling for bargains in imported groceries. Terrific buys on

Cheese

Montrealers are increasingly becoming more knowledgeable about cheese. We travel more than ever and taste better and more interesting cheese. We have gone beyond cheddar and an occasional pasteurized Camembert. Sparse supplies of Italian Mascarpone, layered with basil, or Gorgonzola sell out almost as soon as they arrive in town. Cambazola, a German Brie-type cheese, studded with blue mold, has become extremely popular. Imported goat cheese is now readily available and Quebec-produced goat cheese is quite distinguished.

The Porters talk over old times with The Cheese Shoppe founder, Robert MacConnachie.

The Cheese Shoppe (Mtl)
505 President Kennedy Avenue
Montreal H3A 3H2
849-1232

Days and days of rain in Ireland led
John Porter and his friend to Canadian
shores. They planned to beat it to
Australia if Canada didn't meet their
expectations. Porter was immediately
hired as an assistant to Robert Mac-
Connachie, the owner of the Cheese
Shoppe who had himself emigrated
from Scotland years before. That was
thirty-two years ago. Today Porter owns
the place. But Mr. MacConnachie, now
in his late eighties, still drops by for
a chat from time to time.

The Cheese Shoppe celebrates its
seventy-sixth year in downtown
Montreal . . . having migrated from its
birthplace on Dorchester to its present
Post-Modern home. Time has brought
some changes . . . but the two ancient
brass scales still man the counter.
Made in England in 1775, those scales,
John says, "will turn with a piece of
Kleenex." He adds and subtracts brass
weights to weigh out forty-five pounds
of cheese for a wine and cheese party
for 180. He works closely with the
neighboring Maison des Vins to co-
ordinate wine and cheese.

Cheddar is by far the best-selling
cheese in the shop. Peter dotes on it
. . . visiting Ontario cheese-makers to
find just the right cheddar to age. The
cheese is aged in coolers at the back
of the shop and is shipped all over the
world, especially "down under" and
to Japan.

Porter was the first to introduce the
now-popular German cheese,
Cambazola, to Canada. He thinks the
"absolute champagne of cheese" is
the new Brillador by Brillat Savarin of
France . . . a cow's milk cheese of an
incredible seventy-five percent
butterfat. The Cheese Shoppe carries
an astonishing variety of textures,
tastes, shapes and color in cheese.

Porter swears by the hams, sausages
and bacon brought in from Nichols in
Lennoxville. He says that Nichols'
product is "properly cured – not
injected by needle." John Porter is the
kind of fellow who is not afraid to tell
his customer what to buy. He carries
what he believes to be the best – the
best Scotch smoked salmon,
Summersweet pâtés, smoky kippered
herrings and mackerel. He's a real
charmer . . . complete with an Irish
brogue and a twinkle.

The Cheese Shoppe delivers as far
away as Lake of Two Mountains.
Cheese of the Month Club, gift
certificates and fancy cheese baskets
are always "the right size."

La Foumagerie
4906 Sherbrooke Street West
Westmount H3Z 1H3
482-4100

This bright, cheerful shop in the busy
Victoria Avenue Village boasts over

200 types of cheese. Louis Aird knows his cheese and keeps a solid, classic selection in top condition. Homemade prepared meals like *poulet chasseur* and *canard à l'orange* can be found in the freezer as well as quickly prepared hors d'oeuvres such as tiny pissaladières and seafood profiteroles. There's a well thought-out selection of smoked salmon, pâté and caviar. La Foumagerie specializes in catering wine and cheese parties.

Fromagerie N.D.G.
5727 Monkland Avenue
N.D.G. H4A 1E7
481-7793

This tidy cheese shop carries a well-edited assortment of cheese and cheese biscuits. Brigitte Vaillancourt knows her cheese . . . knows when it's ready to eat and when to keep it for a few days. Some hard-to-find raw-milk cheeses. Also caribou, wild boar and pheasant pâtés.

Le Roi du Fromage
5707 Upper Lachine Road
Montreal H4A 2B1
484-7340

Hidden among the muffler shops of the Upper Lachine Road is this no-nonsense cheese shop. Proprietor Tony Curro carries mostly Italian cheeses for the surrounding Italian neighborhood. Wheels of 1983 Parmigiano-Reggiano decorate the floor. Pecorino, caciotta, blue-veined Gorgonzola, and "little mouthfuls" — *bocconcini* — creamy, fresh balls of cheese. Mascarpone, the very rich triple cream, fresh cheese widely used in Italian cooking, is available five or six times a year. Devotees reserve their Mascarpone ahead of time.

La Tour des Fromages
5502 Jean Talon East
Montreal H1S 1L9
256-3461

Ask Giovanni Conciatori who makes the best bread and he answers "my mother." Who makes the best pasta? "My mother." Giovanni is a connoisseur of all manner of things Italian. A butcher for the last thirty-five years, he has now turned his attention to cheese.

La Tour des Fromages is stacked high with well-aged Parmesans and Romanos. Look for the Romano studded with peppercorns. Counters are filled with fresh, succulent *bocconcini* and mild tumas. Torta di Mascarpone, layered with basil, or Gorgonzola is received from Italy once a month. Tubs of Italian marinated salads and olives to accompany cheese. Giovanni talks about cheese lovingly — with sympathy, with appreciation. The Marcello Mastroianni of cheese.

Ice Cream

Why isn't Montreal an ice cream town? Other frozen cities are crazy for the stuff. In Moscow, where flavors are simplified to vanilla, vanilla and vanilla, ice cream lines are almost as long as the ones for vodka. Some of the big American chains have established somewhat of a cone hold here, but, alas, there are too few native ice cream producers. Old-timers remember Robil's on Bernard and talk lovingly to this day of the taste of a Robil milkshake after matrics.

Indulging in ice cream on a sunny day on the terrace of Bilboquet

La Belle Italienne
5884 Jean Talon East
Montreal H1S 1M2
254-4811

Pink marble everywhere – on the floor, on the counters, on the tables. A welcome pastel oasis off gritty Jean Talon. This gelateria might be in Milan. The shop belongs to Italgelati which makes the ubiquitous little tartufo found in restaurants all over Montreal. Have a dish of gelati and an espresso while deciding what to take home. There's *tiramisù*, the Italian trifle of Mascarpone, chocolate and fruits. Ice creams, ice cream rolls, gelati, granita – a grainy fruit ice – and sorbet-filled

tangerines. And, of course, the tartufo – rich balls of chocolate, vanilla or amaretto ice cream dusted with cocoa.

Bilboquet
1311 Bernard Avenue West
Outremont H2V 1W1
276-0414

A good source of homemade, preservative-free ice creams and sorbets. Also ice cream specialties like napolitain and various *bombes* . . . those wonderfully contrived ice cream extravaganzas. Oranges and lemons filled with sorbet make an elegant finish to a home-cooked meal. Look for the hand-churned ice cream maker in the window.

Crèmerie Roberto Gelateria
2221 Bélanger Street East
Montreal H2G 1C5
374-9844

A gem of a new-fashioned ice cream parlor, tucked away in an Italian-French neighborhood. Counters gleaming with brass details. White, round tables and pretty chairs. Wonderfully built ice cream designs – a kiwi coupe, a gianduiotto, or hazelnut, ice cream. Good-looking ice cream cakes and fruity gelati. A fun place. Take the kids.

It's a tough job, but Xavier can do it.

Food Walks

A gastronomic tour of Montreal is a discovery of the people of this city. They are French-Canadians and English-Canadians. They are Lebanese, West Indian, Jewish, Armenian, Ukrainians, Chinese and on and on. The culinary portfolio of this city is intensely ethnic. Following the food trail has led to the discovery of unknown parts of this city, new friends and interesting things to eat. It's a rewarding way to spend a Saturday morning and to see the city from a food lover's perspective. I've laid out several Food Walks. A good map of Montreal is essential.

Claudette at her stand at the Atwater Market

**Tour One:
The Jean Talon Market**
Métro stop: Jean Talon

Montreal's outdoor markets – colorful, lively, noisy and cluttered – add a special dimension to the shopping life of the city. There are five municipally owned markets. Jean Talon and Atwater are the largest.

Although both are open year-round, spring and fall bring the crowds to enjoy the abundance and the variety of the local produce and the lively market people. The markets expand and contract with the seasons, spreading into the parking lot in the summer and retreating into the market buildings during the winter.

The shops that border the Jean Talon Market deserve the shopper's attention. Pâtisserie Alep, 191 Jean Talon East, makes dozens of kinds of baklava . . . try *kor shokor*, which translates so beautifully into "eat and praise the Lord," or *fatayar sbanik* – dainty pastry triangles filled with spinach.

Cross Jean Talon to the border of the market. There are a number of interesting stores not in the market proper. Shamrock Fish, 7015 Casgrain, the market area's largest fishmonger. Boucherie Chevaline Bernard, 7024 Casgrain – federally inspected, Véronneau brand, western horse meat, and poultry exotica from Ferme du Gourmet, for instance, pheasant,

pigeon, Muscovy duck and chukar partridge. Marché Lakshimi, 7010 Casgrain, provides Indian products to market shoppers.

The heartland of the market is jammed with 130 merchants during the peak season . . . Chez Paul, Chez Louis, Marcel Les Pommes, Nick and Joe's Juicy Fruits. Merchants can be counted on to be friendly, yet aggressive, opinionated and, certainly, passionate. They believe in their radishes, their tomatoes and their eggs. Haggling may or may not get you anywhere. The late, late afternoon, as the market closes, is the most propitious time to give it a shot.

Combine a trip to the Jean Talon Market with visits to the Italian shops on upper St. Laurent Boulevard – Boulangerie Roma, Milano Fruiterie and Faema.

**Tour Two:
The Atwater Market**
Métro stop: Lionel Groulx

The Atwater Market, at the foot of Atwater, is cozy compared with the sprawling Jean Talon Market. The twenty-four merchants who tough out the winter together are joined by sixty-four outdoor companions in the warm months.

Butchers predominate on the second floor of the market building. Gustave Deslauriers specializes in fresh Quebec spring lamb and, that rarity, fresh turkeys. J.P. Maheu — look for the bright red diagram of beef cuts on the wall — will fill freezer orders. Marché Champion has corned beef . . . Boucherie E.B.G., grain-fed fresh turkeys. S.O.S. Boucher does homemade pâtés, marinated meats and French cuts.

Also on the top floor . . . Pasta D'ici . . . fresh pasta, prepared frozen pasta dishes and pasta sauces. Le Vrac du Monde — pounds and pounds of biscuits, flours, dried fruits and nuts. Fromagerie du Deuxième — an exceptional selection of goat cheese from Quebec and France. Boulangerie du Marché offers instant gratification with sticky buns and doughnuts, but, unhappily, bake-off bread, made from frozen dough.

The ground-floor shops are anchored by Poissonnerie Archambault, with its sparkling new counters, and Au Paradis du Fromager, a compact cheese and dairy store specializing in Quebec cheddars . . . look for the sign boasting 300 types of cheese. Raymond's International . . . a clean, friendly place to buy West Indian products . . . a myriad of sauces, legumes, Island vegetables and Island accents.

T. Lauzon is the eggman of the market . . . large, small, brown, white eggs piled high in cardboard crates . . . counters full of poultry parts . . . walls inexplicably adorned with only a huge mounted shark. The takeout window at Restaurant Janot has some of the best french fries in town. Wash them down with local spruce beer.

Cross the street to Distribution Alimentaire Aubut, 155 Atwater — a cavernous cash and carry, friendly to the retail customer. Buy by the case or half case — groceries, soft drinks, paper products.

Tour Three:
de L'Acadie, Dudemaine, Gouin, Laurentien

Montreal's Arab and Lebanese community has settled largely in the northwest sector of the city, at the edge of the Town of Mount Royal and in St. Laurent. The community has

Opposite: Amro Galal says "cheese" at Au Paradis; below, Jean-Paul Deslauriers mans the counter.

spawned a number of the most interesting and appetizing food shops in the city.

Start at Pâtisserie Mahrousé, 1010 Liège Street, just off L'Acadie. Continue north on L'Acadie and you will see a small shopping center just before Sauvé. You've arrived at Phoenicia Adonis, 9590 L'Acadie, one of the very best grocers in the city. Should you want to visit another Arabic food store in the area, continue north along L'Acadie and turn east on Henri Bourassa to Super Marché Suidan, 1545 Henri Bourassa West.

If you still have time, stop for lunch at Restaurant Zahle, 1465 Dudemaine Street . . . straight up L'Acadie, above Henri Bourassa, turn east on

Dudemaine. After relishing Terry's *lahmadjoun*, cross the street to 1560 Dudemaine and see what Nadim Mahrousé has baked at Pâtisserie Dorée.

Still game? Continue north on L'Acadie to Gouin Boulevard, continue west till you reach Pâtisserie de Gascogne, 6095 Gouin Boulevard. Take Laurentien Boulevard south and make a stop at Marché Latina, at 11847 Lachapelle Street, where Laurentien Boulevard turns into Lachapelle.

Opposite and below: Under open skies at the Atwater Market

Tour Four:
Laurier-Bernard

Laurier Avenue and, more recently, Bernard Avenue in Outremont have become delightful walks for the inveterate "foodie."

On Laurier: be dazzled by the food jewels at Lenôtre Paris (at 1050). Next, to Gérard Van Houtte (1042) for some fresh-ground coffee. Cross Park Avenue for lunch or brunch at the charming La Petite Ardoise (222). See what's cooking at Roger Colas (98).

Sneak over to the north side of Laurier and stuff your pockets with May Wests at Stuart Cakes (235), the outlet store

for Culinar. Cross Park Avenue once again and stock up on meat and cheese at Anjou-Québec (1025). A *ficelle* from La Boutique du Pâtissier (1075) completes a visit to Laurier Avenue.

Waddle off to Bernard several streets north. Stop for fresh pasta at Italissimo (615 Bloomfield, corner Bernard). Boulangerie Atlas (1051 Bernard) is a must for delicious Armenian bread and gooey baklava. Perhaps some refreshment at Lester's AAA Delicatessen and Hot Smoked Meat (1057). Organic toothpaste at Mission Santé Thuy (1138). Enthrone yourself at a sidewalk café and watch the mad crowd pass.

More Good Food Walks:

Chinatown, Métro stop: St. Laurent: Plan to visit Chinatown on Sundays when Chinese families do their shopping.

Marché Maisonneuve: A word or two about this public market located at the corner of Ontario and Morgan. Built in 1914 by the renowned Quebec architect Marius Dufresne, the market building is an Art Deco and neoclassic gem — the centerpiece of the Quartier Hochelaga-Maisonneuve. Presiding over the vegetables and flowers is La Maraîchère, a statue by Alfred Laliberté dedicated to the long-suffering wife of the market gardener. History, art, architecture and vegetables.

Index

Foods

93

Index

An invitation:

I'm sure you will have comments, criticisms, corrections, suggestions and, certainly, recommendations. I'd like to hear from you in order to add to and update future editions. Please address your letter to me, care of Tundra Books, 1434 St. Catherine Street West, Montreal, Quebec, H3G 1R4.

Alfred Laliberté's statue of the long-suffering "Market Woman" presides over the Marché Maisonneuve.